Principles of Private Firm Valuation

Founded in 1807, John Wiley & Sons is the oldest independent publishing company in the United States. With offices in North America, Europe, Australia, and Asia, Wiley is globally committed to developing and marketing print and electronic products and services for our customers' professional and personal knowledge and understanding.

The Wiley Finance series contains books written specifically for finance and investment professionals as well as sophisticated individual investors and their financial advisors. Book topics range from portfolio management to e-commerce, risk management, financial engineering, valuation and financial instrument analysis, as well as much more.

For a list of available titles, please visit our Web site at www.WileyFinance.com.

Principles of Private Firm Valuation

STANLEY J. FELDMAN

WILEY

John Wiley & Sons, Inc.

Published by John Wiley & Sons, Inc., Hoboken, New Jersey.
Published simultaneously in Canada.

For general information about our other products and services, please contact our Customer Care Department within the United States at 800-762-2974, outside the United States at 317-572-3993 or fax 317-572-4002.

Wiley also publishes its books in a variety of electronic formats. Some content that appears in print may not be available in electronic books. For more information about Wiley products, visit our web site at www.wiley.com.

Library of Congress Cataloging-in-Publication Data:

Feldman, Stanley J.
    Principles of private firm valuation / by Stanley Jay Feldman.
        p. cm. — (Wiley finance series)
    Includes bibliographical references and index.
    ISBN 0-471-48721-X (cloth)
    1. Small business—Valuation.   I. Title.   II. Series.
    HG4028.V3F44 2005
    658.15'92—dc22

2004025827

Printed in the United States of America.

10   9   8   7   6   5   4   3   2

Contents

Preface

The intended audience for *Principles of Private Firm Valuation* is CPAs, valuation analysts, and CFOs of private firms. Many of the valuation issues these groups deal with are uniquely related to accurately measuring the value of private firms. Several well-known academic and practitioner books deal with the valuation of both public and private businesses. *Principles* added value is that it integrates academic research results with on-the-ground practical experience to provide a more disciplined guidance on how to address several unresolved issues in the arena of private firm valuation:

- Assessing which valuation method is most accurate.
- Estimating the size of the marketability discount; a reduction in value due to the inability to convert to cash at fair market value in a cost-effective way.
- Estimating the value of control and its implication for valuing minority interests in a private firm.
- The influence of taxes on firm value and, specifically, whether S corporations are worth more than equivalent C corporations.
- How best to estimate a private firm's cost of capital.

The purpose of valuing private firms varies. Although a valuation is generally required prior to a private firm being transacted, the majority of private firm valuations are completed for tax-related reasons. For example, equity in a private firm that is part of an estate needs to be valued in order to calculate the estate's tax liability. Similarly, when ownership interests of a private firm are gifted or when they represent a charitable donation, their monetary value needs to be determined, and these valuations typically accompany the donor's tax return. Hence, these valuations are subject to audit by the Internal Revenue Service (IRS).

IRS challenges to business valuations are often adjudicated in Tax Court. As a result, there have been numerous Tax Court rulings that opine on technical valuation issues. Often, these rulings run counter to valuation practice, which places added pressure on valuation analysts to apply methodologies that are consistent with finance theory and objective empirical research. While the role of the Tax Court is to adjudicate, its ability to do so effectively depends on the capacity of valuation experts to articulate the logic underlying their valuation work and to ensure that it is consistent with an accepted scientific knowledge base. Simply arguing that the procedures followed are consistent with accepted practice is not sufficient to sustain a position taken on a technical valuation issue.

The best example of practice versus theory is represented by *Gross v. the Commissioner.*[1] Prior to settlement of this case, it was long-standing practice for S corporations to be valued as though they were C corporations, even though the earnings of the former are taxed only once, at the shareholder level, while the latter's earnings are potentially taxed twice—once at the entity level and again at the shareholder level. Valuation practice recognized that the shareholder tax is typically paid by the S corporation, so for all intents and purposes this tax is equivalent to an entity-level tax paid by a C corporation. Therefore, accepted practice indicated that the value of an S should be based on tax-affecting earnings and assigning a zero value to the S tax benefit. In *Gross,* the IRS argued, and the Tax Court agreed, that taxing an S corporation as if it were a C corporation was incorrect, since the primary benefit of S corporation status is the avoidance of corporate taxes and ignoring this benefit would result in a value that is too low.

The lesson in *Gross* is that no matter what accepted valuation practice happens to be, it will eventually be overruled if it is based on wrongheaded financial analysis. The experience in *Gross* places an increased burden on all valuation professionals since it forces them to predominately base their valuation practices on sound finance and economics principles and somewhat less on accepted practice and past case law. This in turn means that all valuation professionals need to become more familiar with the growing body of academic research related to the valuation of private firms, and, in addition, they need to be more familiar with the research tools that academics use. It is hoped that *Principles* adds to this understanding.

Finally, *Principles* shows how valuation metrics can be used to help owners create more valuable businesses. The same tools that a valuation analyst uses to value a private business can be used to help determine the value contribution from strategic initiatives such as improving inventory management, collecting receivables faster, and increasing the level of net investment. Chapter 2 sets out the managing for value model (MVM), which is designed to measure the value benefits of various strategic initiatives, and Chapter 3 offers a case study that shows how the MVM was used to maximize the value of a private firm.

In the past 25 years, baby boom business owners have created very large, profitable, and, as it turns out, potentially valuable private businesses. Roger Winsby of Axiom Valuation Solutions notes:

Over the next several years, the U.S. economy will experience an unprecedented volume of wealth transfers. Most analysts have focused on the inter-generational wealth transfer from the parents of baby boomers to baby boomers that we are already well into. There is a second, less publicized and less understood transfer that also will take place over the next decade. The entrepreneurial explosion in the U.S. over the last thirty years has resulted in record numbers of small to mid-size, established private businesses (revenues typically in the $1 million to $50 million range). For most of the private businesses started in the 1980s and early 1990s, the owner or owners are now age 50 and over. Just as the baby boomer demographic bulge threatens the solvency of the Social Security system as boomers approach retirement, the private business owner demographic bulge will seriously strain and possibly overwhelm the available supply of buyers and the support infrastructure for business transition and transactions as these owners approach retirement. We call this the business transition tidal wave.[2]

One of the implications of the transition tidal wave is that business owners who expect to sell their businesses need to shift their focus from maximizing after-tax income to maximizing after-tax value. These two objectives are not necessarily the same. Maximizing after-tax income typically means commingling personal and business expenses in an attempt to minimize taxable business income. Maximizing after-tax value, by contrast, requires openness on the expense side that allows a potential buyer to easily discern which expenses are business necessary and which are not. Commingling expenses reduces transparency of firm operations, which will always lead to a reduced business value. The reduction in business value from lack of transparency occurs because a less transparent business represents a more risky business from the vantage point of any potential buyer. In the world of finance, more risk always shows up as less value.

As business owners begin to realize that they need to change their focus to value maximization they will increasingly turn to their most trusted advisor, their CPA, for guidance. For those CPAs not accustomed to addressing transition issues, the MVM will provide valuable insights on how value is created, and it will serve as a platform for sharing these insights with their business owner clients. CPAs who are familiar with MVM will focus on helping their business owner clients to quantify how they can create incremental value by implementing various strategic initiatives and other activities designed to make private firms more transparent.

This book was completed during my Bentley College 2003–2004 sabbatical. It could never have been written without the college's financial support. I owe a debt of gratitude to my university colleagues, to the administrators, and to the Bentley College sabbatical committee who supported my sabbatical application. Many people have contributed to the writing of this book. These include my four research assistants, Todd Feldman, John Edward, Jason Verano, and Abdallah Tannous. Todd Feldman built several of the models used in Chapter 5 on the cost of capital and was a valuable all-around contributor and help throughout the project. John Edward was a major contributor to the development of the control premium model discussed in Chapter 7. Jason Verano and Abdallah Tannous provided invaluable technical and editorial assistance. In addition to these people, I could never have finished the book without the support of my good friend and partner Roger Winsby. Despite all the help I received, I take full responsibility for any errors and/or omissions

STANLEY J. FELDMAN

Wakefield, Massachusetts
February 2005

Principles of Private Firm Valuation

CHAPTER 1

The Value of Fair Market Value

P rivate firms can be valued under multiple standards of value, the most notable standard being *fair market value* (FMV). The FMV standard has several important implications for establishing the value of a private firm. These include identifying the circumstances under which a business entity is being valued, the quality of the information that various valuation models require, and a logical framework for establishing the basis of value. This discussion is important because the models and metrics in this book are designed to establish a private firm's FMV. Therefore, understanding the meaning of FMV and all that it implies is crucial to understanding the steps necessary to determine a private firm's FMV. The IRS applies the FMV standard to all gift, estate, and income tax matters. IRS Revenue Ruling 59–60 in part states:

> *FMV is the price at which the property would change hands between a willing buyer and a willing seller when the former is not under any compulsion to buy and the latter is not under any compulsion to sell, both parties having reasonable knowledge of the relevant facts. Court decisions frequently state in addition that the hypothetical buyer and seller are assumed to be able, as well as willing to trade and to be well informed about the property and concerning the market for such property.*[1]

Other valuation standards include *liquidation value* and *investment value.*[2] The Financial Accounting Standards Board (FASB) uses the term *fair value* when referring to financial reporting standards that require booking assets and liabilities at FMV. Since FMV is associated with a large body of case law developed in the context of tax regulation that may not be relevant for financial reporting purposes, the FASB concluded that the fair value naming convention was appropriate under the circumstances. However, the name difference does not imply that there is any substantive difference in the concepts. Other standards of value differ from FMV in that they do not incorporate all of the criteria that an FMV standard requires. Therefore, FMV can be thought of as a baseline value standard with other value standards being distinguished by lack of one or more of the attributes that define the FMV standard.

FAIR MARKET VALUE: THE MEANING FOR THE VALUE OF PRIVATE FIRMS

Three features embody FMV:

1. The notion of a hypothetical transaction that leads to the establishment of an exchange value.
2. Willing buyer and willing seller.
3. Reasonably informed parties to a transaction.

Hypothetical Transaction

When determining the value of a public firm, one can always defer to the financial markets for guidance. If we consider a firm that is all equity financed, has a recently established share price of $10, and 1 million shares outstanding, then the firm's market capitalization, and the firm's value, is $10 million. Therefore, to determine the value of an equity interest in a public firm, one does not need to assume a hypothetical transaction; one only needs to view the most current share price.

Since a private firm by definition does not have any economic interest traded in a market, the value must be established under an assumption of a hypothetical transaction. The outcome of a hypothetical transaction is an exchange price that reflects the price that would result in an exchange between willing and informed parties, and in this sense the exchange would be fair. Therefore the hypothetical transaction is assumed to mimic the process that would occur in a market between willing informed buyers and willing informed sellers. This does not mean that a market price would be established, but rather that the process of arriving at exchange value or price would be the same as would occur if the participants were operating in a market.

The notion of a fair exchange flows directly from the concept of parties to the transaction being fully informed. If both parties have the same information and act on it, then the resulting price must be fair. Markets are generally believed to provide exchange prices that are fair because it is assumed that all parties and/or their agents have equivalent information about the risks and opportunities that are expected to impact the performance of the firm whose economic interest is being transacted. Thus, transaction prices would not be fair if groups of participants were disadvantaged in the sense that their access to information is limited or the quality of what they have access to is substantively deficient. Transaction prices are generally believed to be consistent with FMV when transactions take place in markets governed by regulations designed to maximize accurate and timely disclosure of critical financial data and other performance information. Therefore, in markets characterized by asymmetric information, transaction prices will not meet the FMV standard.

Willing Buyer and Willing Seller

This characteristic means that potential buyers and sellers are not forced to transact. Each party can withdraw and, in most cases, can do so without a penalty. In contrast, a liquidation value standard requires that the selling party transact and accept the best price. In this case, sellers cannot withdraw and therefore have no recourse as they would under the FMV standard. Moreover, *willing* also implies that market participants have the means to be parties to an exchange. Calculating the FMV of a private firm assumes that hypothetical buyers have the financial wherewithal and sellers have the legal right to sell the interests in question.

Reasonably Informed

This attribute means that buyers and sellers are cognizant of an entity's true cash flow and also have expectations of future performance consistent with those held by knowledgeable market participants. Let us consider the cash flow issue first. Assume that Company X reported no profit in each of the past five years. Would having this knowledge meet the reasonably informed criteria? The answer is no if, after disentangling the firm's financial statements, one established that the firm indeed made a profit in each of the past five years, and a fairly large one at that. How could this happen? If analysis of the firm's financial statements showed that lack of reported profit was the result of the owner receiving a salary in excess of what an outside executive would normally receive for doing the same job, or payments to family member employees far in excess of what unrelated people would earn for the same work, or the existence of other expenses like club fees that were purely discretionary, then one might reasonably conclude that adjusting reported expenses for these excesses would result in the firm earning a profit. Although the financial statements were accurate in this example, being reasonably informed means more than being informed about the accuracy of the financial statements. *Reasonably informed,* in the context of FMV, means that market participants are knowledgeable about the true financial condition of the firm.

Being reasonably informed also means that parties to a transaction have performance expectations that are fully consistent with those held by knowledgeable market participants. Since the hypothetical transaction that informed parties engage in is intended to mimic the information processing that ordinarily takes place in a market environment, it follows that informed investors in a private transaction would also require, at a minimum, the quantity and quality of information that would normally be available to them if they were engaging in a market-based transaction.

Finally, the reasonably informed criterion also means that participants and/or their agents can accurately process disclosed information and rationally act on it. If this were not the case, then accurate disclosures about the current and expected future performance of the transacted entity would have no practical meaning. The assumption of rational participants in a transaction that underlies FMV can best be appreciated by considering the logic often presented for the difference in value between a controlling and a minority economic interest.

FMV AND THE VALUES OF CONTROLLING AND MINORITY INTERESTS

A *minority owner* is one who exchanges cash for the right to receive future cash flow, but who has no influence over how the assets of the firm that produce the cash flow are managed and/or financed. A *control owner* has the right to alter how the assets are used and financed, and also has control over the size and timing of any cash distributions. Because minority owners have no control over cash distributions, it is often believed that minority ownership in a private corporation has little or no value.

To understand the full implications of this last point, consider the following hypothetical transaction: A firm's control owner desires to sell a minority interest in the firm. The minority investor exchanges cash in return for a minority interest because he believes that he will receive regular distributions from the firm. Once the transaction is completed, the control owner raises his compensation to the point where the firm can no longer make any distributions. Knowing that a control owner can do this, the question is, why would anybody purchase a minority interest in a private firm for anything more than a trivial sum? Because of this possibility, it is often concluded that a minority interest is worth much less than a controlling interest in a private firm.

The problem with this logic is that it is inconsistent with the FMV standard. Indeed, under the preceding scenario, a transaction would never take place. The reason is that FMV assumes a rational buyer. That is, under what conditions would a rational informed investor purchase a minority interest in a private firm? Surely no rational investor would purchase any minority shares under the preceding conditions. Since no transaction would take place, minority discounts cannot be based on this logic. What logic is implied under an FMV standard that offers guidance about the size of a minority discount in a hypothetical transaction? Although, FMV does not stipulate the conditions under which a minority interest is transacted, it does imply that a rational and informed buyer would never purchase a minority interest in a private firm unless there were enforceable oversight provisions and associated financial penalties for noncompliance by the control owner. Oversight provisions might include a board seat and the ability to audit the books on a regular basis. While oversight is critical to the minority owner being kept reasonably informed about the operations of the firm, the minority owner still has no control over who receives cash distributions, how much they receive, and the timing of when the cash distributions are made. Nevertheless, there are a number of ways rational minority owners could protect themselves from potential abuses by a control owner. Such protections will be a function of the fact pattern that is unique to each valuation circumstance. The point here is not to articulate what these protections might be, but rather to suggest that a rational acquirer of a minority interest would demand such protections before purchasing a minority interest. This discussion suggests that determining the FMV of a minority interest under the assumption of a hypothetical transaction implies that reasonable protections are in place so the control owner cannot siphon off cash at the expense of the minority owner.

FMV AND STRATEGIC VALUE

FMV requires that participants are reasonably informed about the risks and opportunities of the property in question and are also knowledgeable about the factors that shape the market in which the entity is expected to transact. This implies that the business is being valued on a going-concern basis. For example, assume that a textile firm recently sold for $1,000. The acquirer plans to use the assets of the firm to produce steel, and is willing to pay a premium over its value as a textile firm to ensure that his offer is accepted. Is $1,000 the textile firm's FMV? The answer is no. The reason is that the price does not reflect the value of the firm as a textile producer but rather as a steel company. Thus, when FMV is the standard of value in a hypothetical transaction, the standard assumes that the entity being transacted will continue to operate as it had before the transaction. This follows from the definition of FMV, which states that the buyer and seller are well informed about the "property and the market for such property."[3] In the example, the market for this property is the market for the textile firm, and hence its FMV is based on this.

Strategic or investment value emerges when an acquirer desires to use the assets of the acquired firm in a specific way and this use gives rise to cash flows in addition to those that can be expected from the firm being operated in its going-concern state. To see the difference between investment value and FMV, consider the following example. A local insurance agent would like to sell her agency. An informed potential buyer who desires to run the agency much like the seller is willing to pay $1,000 for the agency. The seller believes this price is consistent with the firm's FMV. A nationally recognized financial services firm has decided to purchase local agencies all over the country as part of a roll-up strategy designed to reduce the costs of managing local agencies as well as to sell additional insurance products to the client bases of purchased agencies. The nationally recognized financial services firm is a strategic buyer. This buyer is always willing to pay more than a buyer who desires to run the business like the seller. The reason a strategic buyer will pay a premium over FMV is that the buyer expects the combined businesses to generate more cash flow than they could produce as two stand-alone entities. The price established by the strategic buyer is not the firm's FMV because the exchange value is not based on the business as it is currently configured. FMV does include a control premium; however, it is only partially related to the premium established via a strategic acquisition. In a strategic purchase the control premium is made up of two components—the value of pure control and the synergy value that emerges from the combination that is captured by the seller in the competitive bidding process. In the preceding example, the strategic buyer is willing to pay a premium over the value of the agencies cash flows for the right to manage and finance the assets to ensure that the expected cash flows from the going concern accrue to the owner. This is the value of pure control, and it is based on the risks and opportunities of the entity as a going concern. The second part of the premium emerges because of the synergy value created by the combination. This portion is not part of the acquired firm's FMV. Therefore, investment value is effectively equal to the FMV of the acquired firm plus the captured synergy value.

This last result bears directly on the calculation of a firm's minority equity FMV. Without reviewing the arithmetic of translating a reported premium for control to the implied discount for a minority interest, we simply note that a 50 percent control premium translates to a 33 percent minority discount.[4] In practice, a valuation analyst will typically arrive at a firm's control equity FMV and then reduce it by the implied minority discount to arrive at the firm's minority equity FMV. To see this, let us assume the valuation analyst arrived at a control value of $150 for an all-equity firm. From a number of control premium studies, the analyst calculated a median control premium of 50 percent, then calculated the implied minority discount of

33 percent. This means that the minority equity FMV is $100, which amounts to a 33 percent discount to its control FMV of $150. However, the discount calculated was based on a control premium that is likely made up of both a pure control premium and a synergy option. If the reported 50 percent control premium is divided evenly between pure control and the synergy option, the minority discount would be 20 percent and the minority value of equity for FMV purposes would be $120.[5] Thus, using raw control premium data to calculate a minority discount will overstate the discount and result in a minority equity value that is too low. In turn, the overstatement of diminution in value will be greater the larger the synergy option is relative to the total control value. Chapter 7 addresses valuing control and sets out a method for estimating the value of pure control.

SUMMARY

In most instances, the standard of value used to value private firms is FMV. Unlike public firms, whose prices are established in organized markets, the value of a private firm's equity must be estimated under the assumption of a hypothetical transaction. The notion of a hypothetical transaction under which a firm's FMV is established requires that one articulate the implications of the standard to establishing value. FMV requires the valuation analyst to assume that the parties to a transaction are reasonably informed about the relevant facts. This criterion means that the valuation analyst must use all the information that a reasonably informed investor would use to arrive at FMV. In other words, FMV is established for a private firm when the process used to establish value effectively mimics what would occur if the transaction took place in a properly regulated public market environment. Market prices are assumed to be fair because parties to a market transaction have equivalent information, so neither buyer nor seller is disadvantaged.

This chapter also addressed the implication of FMV for valuing minority interest; namely, the valuation of a minority interest assumes that the minority owner has some protections in place that limit potential abuse by the control owner. Valuing control is taken up in Chapter 7.

CHAPTER 2

Creating and Measuring the Value of Private Firms

Owners of private firms manage their businesses to increase their after-tax profit. Unfortunately, this may not always translate to maximizing the value of their firms. In this chapter, we introduce a framework that more closely ties the desire to increase after-tax profits to maximizing the value of the firm. We call this framework the *managing for value model* (MVM). While models of this sort are often used to quantify whether business strategies undertaken by public firms create value for shareholders, it is also a powerful tool for evaluating whether the business decisions of control owners result in increasing their private wealth. When applying the model, owners immediately realize actions taken that might increase revenue and even increase after-tax profit may not lead to an increase in firm value, and in some cases actually result in a decrement in value. They, of course, wonder how this is possible. It is, to say the least, counterintuitive, but nevertheless, it is an outcome that often emerges. The question is: What are the circumstances that give rise to this result? The answer varies, but in general it emerges when a particular business strategy yields an after-tax rate of return that, while positive and large, is nevertheless not large enough. This means that the after-tax rate of return is lower than the financial costs to create it, resulting in a decrement in firm value.

To see this, assume a firm borrows $100 at 10 percent and promises to pay back the loan at the end of one year. The firm invests the $100 and only earns 8 percent, so at the end of the year the investment is worth $108. However, the firm promised to pay the lender $110 at the end of the year. Where does the firm get the additional $2? Simple, either the firm sells off some assets, issues some stock, or borrows the $2 from another financial source. In any case, the owner is $2 poorer and the firm is worth $2 less. Thus, earning a positive return does not necessarily mean that the firm and the owner are better off. Indeed, using earnings as a measure of success may lead management to take actions that destroy, rather than enhance, the value of the firm. Employing the MVM reduces the likelihood that this will happen.

The MVM sets down procedures that help business owners and managers understand the options available to create competitive advantage and maximize the value of the firms they both own and manage. Owners create value by managing current firm assets, adding new assets, and altering how both current and future assets are financed. Determining how to deploy the firm's current and future assets is the domain of business strategy. How the asset base is financed is the domain of financial policy. This discussion gives rise to the first principle of managing for value:

> Principle 1. *Owners maximize the value of what they own when a firm's financial policies are properly aligned with the firm's business strategies. This occurs when the value of expected after-tax cash flows from a firm's assets is maximized and the firm's after-tax financing costs are minimized.*

In the section that follows, the basic components of the MVM are discussed and analyzed. In Chapter 3 the MVM is applied to a real-world case involving Richard Fox, the CEO and a significant owner of Frier Manufacturing.

THE MVM

The MVM is summarized in Figure 2.1. As one moves counterclockwise around the outer circle, the degree of strategic management intensifies. Less active strategic management implies that owner/managers are optimizing the cash flows from the assets in place at the optimal capital structure. Optimal capital structure is the debt-to-equity ratio that yields a maximum value for the cash flows from assets in place. When management becomes more active, it adds assets and continues to finance them at the optimal capital structure. When net fixed capital and sales grow at their historical rates, management is undertaking an active strategy designed to exploit market opportunities that have been previously identified. Examples include pricing initiatives intended to increase market share or sales increases of previously introduced new products. The value that emerges from implementing these actions is known as *going-concern value*, and it reflects the continuation of past business decisions into the future.

Highly active strategic management begins when the firm's owners decide to alter the basis of competition in some significant way. Such changes might include a business restructuring designed to reduce costs, lower prices, and increase market share in each of the markets served, developing new products and services, and/or entering new markets. Each of these changes represents a significant change in a firm's strategy, and each

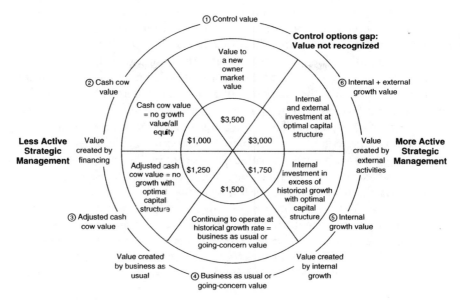

FIGURE 2.1 The Value Circle Framework

usually requires the firm to increase internal investments or net new capital expenditures beyond what it has historically done. Depending on the strategic thrust, management may decide that buying is cheaper than building and therefore decide to commit itself to an acquisition or series of acquisitions. Such external investments might be accompanied by divestitures of business units that no longer fit with the firm's core business strategy.

MEASURING THE CONTRIBUTION OF STRATEGY TO FIRM VALUE

Figure 2.1 shows that a firm's value is the sum of the values created by various strategic initiatives. The aggregation of these values is equal to the value of the firm, which is also equal to the sum of the market value of the firm's equity plus the market value of its debt. Moving counterclockwise, the no-growth value is made up of the value of assets in place. This value is equivalent to capitalizing the firm's current cash flow by its equity cost of capital. In this case, each year's gross investment equals annual depreciation, so the assets in place are always sufficiently maintained to provide the required cash flow. Thus, if a firm's annual after-tax cash flow is $1 million and the firm's cost of equity capital is 10 percent, then the firm has an equity market value of $10.0 million ($1 million ÷ 0.10). If the firm has 1 million shares outstanding, then each share is worth $10. This can be thought of as its *cash cow value* since the firm would be generating cash that would not be reinvested but would be distributed to owners.[1]

By altering the firm's capital structure, the cash cow value can potentially be enhanced. Keep in mind that total firm value is equal to the market value of equity plus the market value of debt. Interest costs are tax deductible and dividends from equity shares are not. Therefore, if a firm can issue $1 of debt and buy back a $1 of equity, thus refinancing the asset base, its tax bill will be reduced. This reduction will occur each year over the life of the debt, and thus the present value of these tax savings is the value increment associated with this refinancing. These tax benefits come at a cost, however. As the firm increases its leverage, the probability of bankruptcy also increases. As long as the present value of additional debt adds more value through its tax benefit than the value decrement that occurs because of the increased probability of bankruptcy, then adding debt will increase firm value. The optimal capital structure will emerge when these two offsetting factors are equal.[2] The firm's optimal capital structure, its optimal debt-to-equity ratio, is located at the minimum (maximum) point of the firm's cost of capital (value) curve, as shown in Figure 2.2.

The extension of the optimal capital structure concept to S corporations was indirectly offered by Merton Miller in his 1976 presidential address to the American Finance Society. In this address he showed how leverage affects firm value in the presence of both corporate and personnel taxes. The Miller model shows that even if a firm does not pay an entity-level tax, like an S corporation, leverage can still create value.

It is often thought that a private firm cannot alter its capital structure cost effectively and easily. This view is not correct. In addition to commercial banks, there are other sources of lending to private firms, including private investor groups such as small business investment companies (SBICs), which are sponsored by the SBA to provide debt as well as equity financing. The sources of financing have been growing rapidly over the past 15 years, reflecting the growth in the number and value of private firms. The basic factors determining the ability of a private firm to refinance have not changed, however. The greater the transparency of a firm's operations and the more sustainable the firm's cash flow, the greater the chances that a refinancing strategy at competitive rates of interest can be achieved.

Determining the optimal capital structure is a complicated exercise and beyond the scope of this chapter. For the moment, let us assume that management has determined that the optimal capital structure is 50 percent debt and 50 percent equity and, as a result, the adjusted cash cow value is $1,250 million. This adjusted value less the cash cow value of $1,000 million, represents the value created through financial restructuring.

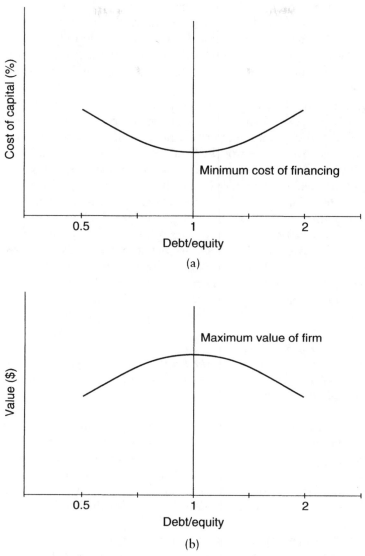

FIGURE 2.2 Value Curve

The business-as-usual value, or *going-concern value,* is a product of the firm's sales and capital needs growing at recent historical rates. These activities are financed at the firm's optimal capital structure and reflect the fact that management does not expect the future to deviate in any important way from the past. Say management plans to increase capital expenditures in excess of depreciation to take advantage of identified growth opportunities. These new investments are expected to create additional value for the firm. Going-concern value is calculated to be $1,500 million, with the difference between it and the adjusted cash cow value, $1,250 million, representing the additional value created by the net increase in capital expenditures.

There are several reasons why the going-concern value exceeds the adjusted cash cow value. The first is that the going-concern value reflects strategic opportunities, and therefore the net new investment is expected to yield a rate of return in excess of the firm's cost of capital, which by definition does not occur in an adjusted cash cow environment. This implies that the value of the incremental after-tax cash flows exceeds the value of the net new investment required to generate them. This emerges either because the incremental after-tax cash flows are sufficiently large and/or the increments created last for a sufficiently long enough time to validate the investment made. The period over which a firm is expected to earn rates of return that exceed its cost of capital is known as the *competitive advantage* period. Because competition has become more intense across all industries, it is difficult to sustain what economists call *monopoly rents* for an extended period. This insight leads to the second principle of managing for value:

Principle 2. *All else equal, the greater the degree of competition in any served market, the shorter the length of the competitive advantage period the firm faces and the less likely that any strategic initiative will create firm value.*

As principle 2 becomes operative and its effects visible, the greater the likelihood that owners of private firms begin to entertain and host strategic initiatives designed to defend, and potentially alter, the basis of competition in served markets. In addition, owners may consider developing new products and services and/or enter new markets where the firm can more effectively create barriers to entry, thereby increasing the length of the competitive advantage period.

When it becomes apparent to owners that they must alter the way they do business in order to sustain their current position, they begin to explore the implications of this new reality in terms of internal and external investment options and to select those that enhance the firm's competitive position and create a more valuable firm. Internal options include developing new product lines, investing in research and development (R&D), initiating programs to cut overhead and variable costs, opening new markets for existing products, and increasing market share in served markets for existing products and services. When the value of these additional activities is added to going-concern value, the value of the firm, or its internal growth value, rises to $1,750 million.

Keep in mind that the internal growth value can be lower than the going-concern value. This occurs when the present value of costs of internal investments exceeds the present value of the cash flows produced by these investments. We gave a simple example of this phenomenon at the beginning of this chapter. We now want to formalize it as an operating principle and give an example of it at work.

> Principle 3. *A firm should undertake a net new investment only when the expected rate of return exceeds the cost of capital required to finance it. This will occur when the present value of expected cash flows exceeds the present value of net new investments.*

How an investment strategy can destroy value is exemplified by the 1980s experience of oil company executives who blindly committed large sums of capital to finance oil exploration and development when it was clear that such investments destroyed firm value. While this example concerns itself with public firms, many private firms were involved in oil exploration as well during this time. They, like their public firm counterparts, believed that the high price of a barrel of oil was, in itself, sufficient to undertake the large expenditure that oil exploration required. As it turns out, principle 3 was violated, and this led to a restructuring of the oil industry and to a major restructuring across other industries as well. This occurred because it became clear that many firms had been violating principle 3, which in turn offered opportunities to entrepreneurs to purchase these firms, divest operations that were not adding value, and thus create a more valuable entity. Put differently, entrepreneurs purchased firms for less than they were worth and, by suspending operations that were not creating value, were able to create a more valuable entity.

When Strategy Destroys Value: The Case of the Oil Industry

In the early 1980s, the corporate value of integrated oil firms was less than the market value of their oil reserves, their primary assets. The question arose, how could such a mispricing occur given that the major oil companies are so widely followed by the investor community? A 1985 research report prepared by Bernard Picchi of Salomon Brothers provided the answer. The report indicated that the 30 largest oil firms earned less than their cost of capital of about 10 percent on their oil exploration and development expenditures.[3]

Estimates of the average ratio of the present value of future net cash flows of discoveries, extensions, and enhanced recovery to expenditures for exploration and development for the industry ranged from less than 0.6 to slightly more than 0.9, depending on the method used and the year. In other words, on average, the oil industry was receiving somewhere between 60 and 90 cents for each dollar invested. The corporate value of these firms reflected the sum of the market value of oil reserves minus the value destroyed by investing in oil exploration and development. Therefore, by undertaking internal investments that destroyed value, stock prices of these oil firms were lower than they would have been had they immediately terminated most of their exploration and development activities. The strategic implications of this analysis are that it was cheaper to obtain oil reserves through buying the assets of a competitor than it was to invest internally and explore. In this way, the capital markets provided incentives for firms to make strategic adjustments that were not stimulated by competitive forces in the international markets for oil. In the end, shareholder wealth increased significantly as some oil firms merged and others restructured. The events that transpired and the shareholder wealth gains that materialized are described in the following article.

RESTRUCTURING OF THE OIL INDUSTRY

Gains to the shareholders in the Gulf/Chevron, Getty/Texaco, and DuPont/Conoco mergers, for example, totaled more than $17 billion. Much more is possible. In a 1986 MIT working paper, "The 217 Agency Costs of Corporate Control: The Petroleum Industry," Jacobs estimates total potential gains of approximately $200 billion from eliminating the inefficiencies in 98 petroleum firms as of December 1984.

Recent events indicate that actual takeover is not necessary to induce the required adjustments:

> The Phillips restructuring plan, brought about by the threat of takeover, involved substantial retrenchment and return of resources to shareholders, and the result was a gain of $1.2 billion (20 percent) in Phillips's market value. The company repurchased 53 percent of its stock for $4.5 billion in debt, raised its dividend 25 percent, cut capital spending, and initiated a program to sell $2 billion of assets.

> Unocal's defense in the Mesa tender offer battle resulted in a $2.2 billion (35 percent) gain to shareholders from retrenchment and return of resources to shareholders. Unocal paid out 52 percent of its equity by repurchasing stock with a $4.2 billion debt issue and reduced costs and capital expenditures.

The voluntary restructuring announced by ARCO resulted in a $3.2 billion (30 percent) gain in market value. ARCO's restructuring involved a 35 to 40 percent cut in exploration and development expenditures, repurchase of 25 percent of its stock for $4 billion, a 33 percent increase in its dividend, withdrawal from gasoline marketing and refining east of the Mississippi, and a 13 percent reduction in its workforce.

The announcement of the Diamond-Shamrock reorganization in July 1985 provides an interesting contrast to the others because the company's market value fell 2 percent on the announcement day. Because the plan results in an effective increase in exploration and capital expenditures and a reduction in cash payouts to investors, the restructuring does not increase the value of the firm. The plan involved reducing cash dividends by 76 cents per share (a cut of 43 percent), creating a master limited partnership to hold properties accounting for 35 percent of its North American oil and gas production, paying an annual dividend of 90 cents per share in partnership shares, repurchasing 6 percent of its shares for $200 million, selling 12 percent of its master limited partnership to the public, and *increasing* its expenditures on oil and gas exploration by $100 million per year.

External Strategies: Acquisitions

The oil industry case suggests that external investment strategies should always be seriously considered. External strategies include acquisitions and various types of divestitures of nonstrategic assets. In general, an acquisition should be considered when there are synergies between the acquirer and the target firm. In this case, the value of the combined firms should exceed the sum of the market values of each as stand-alone businesses. This difference is termed *acquisition* or *synergy value.* If the price paid for a firm exceeds its current market price, the difference being termed the *target premium,* then the net value created by the acquisition is the difference between the synergy value and the target premium. The value of the combined firms is then equal to the value of each firm as a stand-alone plus the difference between the acquisition value and the target premium. Keep in mind that a target's value not only reflects the additional cash flows that are expected to emerge as a result of the combination, but any options that the combination may create to be exercised in the future if circumstances develop that support such execution. Because such strategic options are difficult to quantify, they are often overlooked when valuing an acquisition. This, of course, would be a mistake, since it necessarily leads to undervaluing any acquisition undertaken.

The value created by an acquisition can be seen by considering the case of Firm A, which has a current stand-alone market value of $100, and Firm T, which has a current stand-alone value of $50. Firm A believes that it can manage Firm T's assets and create additional value of $25. This $25 is the synergy value. If Firm A paid a $10 premium for Firm T's assets (i.e., paid $60 for them), the combined value of Firms A and T would equal $115 (stand-alone Firm A value of $100 + stand-alone Firm T value of $50 + $25 synergy value − $60 Firm T cost = $115). Firm A is willing to pay a premium for Firm T's assets because Firm A can create additional value that exceeds the target premium by being able to control how Firm T's assets are to be deployed. Hence, the target premium is also known as the *control premium*. This acquisition creates $15 of value for the owners of Firm A because they paid $60 for something that is worth $75. Keep in mind that the $25 in value that Firm A's owners believe can be created may reflect incremental direct cash flows that emerge from the combination—removal of redundant administrative costs, for example, as well as options to do things in the future that would not be possible or financially feasible without control of Firm T's assets. These options might include Firm T patents not in use and R&D programs. Keep in mind that these options are not part of the additional cash flows expected to emerge because of the combination, but represent cash flows that emerge only if the patents not in use, for example, are exercised at some future time. This leads to principle 4:

> Principle 4. *An acquisition should not be undertaken if the price paid exceeds the incremental value that the acquisition is designed to create. Any incremental value should reflect both the direct expected cash flows and any options embedded in the assets being acquired.*

Acquisition strategies are often thought to be the sole domain of public firms. This is not only untrue, but private firms often have more to gain by pursuing acquisition strategies than do their public firm counterparts. The reason relates to the influence of firm size on value, as attested by the following case study.

CASE STUDY: FPI Restructures to Create Value

Joel owns FPI, a financial planning organization. FPI was recently valued at $36 million, or three times its past 12 months of revenue of $12 million. The financial planning industry is fragmented and is made up of a large number of smaller producers. John has approached Joel and is willing to help him finance a series of acquisitions. The idea is to purchase a series of smaller firms for about three times their annual revenue, integrate the firms, and sell the larger entity to a financial services firm that is willing to pay a multiple well in excess of 3 for the integrated firm. John has studied recent acquisitions in other industries and has noticed larger firms sell for much larger multiples of revenue than smaller firms.

This observation leads John to initiate a strategy that leverages Joel's operating experience and an investor's willingness to pay a premium for larger firms. John convinces Joel that purchasing two firms with annual revenue of $12 million each and integrating them with Joel's firm will create a combined entity that is worth more than it costs to create. Total revenue of the combined entity is $36 million, and at three times revenue, its value is $108 million. John and Joel know that Financial Services Inc. (FSI) has been looking to acquire a financial planning firm that is sufficiently large to make an impact on the performance of FSI. John and Joel's new firm provides the size that FSI is looking for, in addition to a wealthy customer base to whom FSI can sell its various products and services. FSI is willing to pay four times revenue for John and Joel's firm, which means they and their 20 minority shareholders increase their wealth by $36 million (4 × $36 − 3 × $36).

Acquisitions in the private market often make sense when an industry is fragmented and made up of a number of small producers. By aggregating these businesses and integrating their operations, the value of this new combined entity has a value that exceeds the sum of the values of the two businesses as stand-alone operations. This occurs even if there are no additional cash flows that result from the combination. The reason is that the combined entity is less risky than the risk of each entity separately. This means that the cost of capital of the combination is lower than the cost of capital of each business as a stand-alone operation.

An example would be helpful. Suppose Firms A and B have after-tax earnings of $100 in perpetuity and each has a cost of capital of 10 percent. The value of each firm is therefore $1,000 ($100 ÷ 0.10). The two firms combined have a value of $2,000, but this is understating the value of the combination, since the new larger firm with an after-tax cash flow of $200 also has a lower cost of capital, 9 percent. This lower cost of capital means that the combination is worth $2,222, or an additional $222 in value simply because of size.[4]

In addition to size, there are at least two other reasons why a larger firm will sell at a higher multiple of revenue than a smaller firm. The first relates to scale. The time and effort it takes to integrate a larger target is often as great as it is for a smaller target. Hence, for the same effort and cost, the benefits are greater for a larger entity than for a smaller entity. Second, the synergy options are often far greater when the purchased entity is larger. More new products and services can be sold through a larger organization than a smaller one, and therefore the after-tax cash flow per employee is likely to be far greater as well. In addition to these factors, if an acquirer is a public firm, it may be able to pay a higher premium than an acquiring private firm for a target's cash flow. The reason is that the public firm has additional purchasing capacity, since it is valued at a premium relative to the value of a comparable private firm. That is, equity shares of public firms are more liquid than the shares of comparable private firms. This means that public firm shares sell at higher multiples of revenue than the shares of comparable private firms. This increased liquidity emerges because owners of public firms can sell their shares cost-effectively and at prices that fully reflect expectations of informed investors regarding the firm's underlying risk and earnings potential. Therefore, if a public firm can purchase a private firm in the same industry at a revenue multiple of 4 and then have the public market revalue this purchased revenue at 5, the acquisition creates value for the shareholders of the public firm.

The arithmetic is simple and compelling. As indicated in the FPI case, FSI pays $144 million for $36 million of revenue. Once the acquisition is announced, the value of the financial services firm will increase by $36 million, or the difference between $180 million (5 × $36 million) and $144 million. This upward revaluation occurs solely because the public firm is a more liquid entity. This result leads to principle 5:

> Principle 5. *Given two firms in the same industry, one public and the other private, the public firm will always pay more for a target than a comparable private firm, all else equal.*

External Strategies: Divestitures

In addition to acquisitions, owners of private firms may decide to sell only part of the business. This type of business restructuring can take several forms: divestitures, equity carve-outs, and spin-offs being the most notable. As shown in Figure 2.3, a divestiture is the sale of a division or a portion of a firm in return for cash and/or marketable securities.

The sale may be to another firm or it may be a management buyout (MBO). When the sale is financed with a significant amount of debt, the transaction is termed a *leveraged buyout* (LBO). If the division's sale price exceeds its value to the parent as a stand-alone business, then the divestiture increases the market value of the selling firm by this difference. To see this, consider Firm A, which is made up of two divisions, each valued at $50. Division 2 is sold for $60, a $10 premium over its intrinsic value. After the sale, Firm A is worth $110 (division 1 = $50 + division 2's sale proceeds = $60), or $10 more than before the sale. This example gives rise to principle 6:

> Principle 6. *If a division or line of business of a private firm is worth more to outsiders (external market) than it is internally, then the entity should be sold and the funds received should be deployed in a business line where the owner and/or the firm has a measurable competitive advantage, thus ensuring that the value of the firm is maximized.*

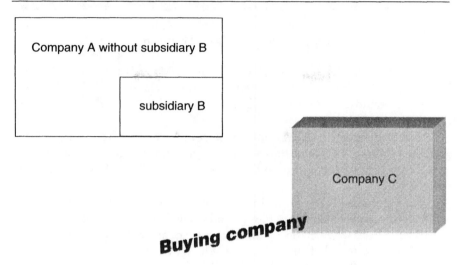

(a) *Company before Divestiture*

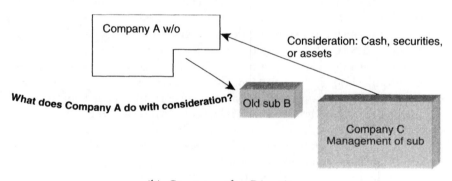

(b) *Company after Divestiture*

FIGURE 2.3 Structure of a Divestiture

By John Carreyrou and Martin Peers
Staff Reporters of the *Wall Street Journal*

Vivendi Universal SA rejected Metro-Goldwyn-Mayer Inc.'s $11.5 billion bid for its U.S. film and TV businesses as too low and refused to bow to MGM's demand for more due diligence information, according to people familiar with the matter.

Vivendi's rebuff of MGM's ultimatum comes days after it dismissed Liberty Media Corp.'s demand for exclusive negotiations, signaling the French company's resolve not to be bullied by bidders in the high-profile media auction.

The move also shows Vivendi is being ambitious in the price it is seeking for the assets, which include the Hollywood studio Universal Pictures, the Universal theme parks, a television production studio, and cable TV networks.

Though still saddled with a large debt load of some €13 billion, Vivendi believes it can afford to be picky because it has restructured its debt to be able to last well into 2004 without a cash injection.

The company's confidence also has been buoyed by the recent stock market rally, which it thinks could allow it to proceed with an initial public offering of the businesses should bidders' offers remain underwhelming.

MGM bid $11.2 billion for the businesses in the auction's first round last month, putting it at the upper level of bids received. Other bidders included John Malone's Liberty Media, General Electric Co.'s NBC, Viacom Inc., and an investor group led by former Seagram CEO Edgar Bronfman Jr.

Seeking an edge, MGM earlier this week told Vivendi in a letter that it was prepared to raise its offer to $11.5 billion on the condition that it receive more information about the businesses by next Monday, including details about agreements governing how Vivendi's cable channels are carried by cable and satellite TV systems. While Vivendi wasn't happy with MGM's demands for extra information, which ran to almost 20 pages, one person familiar with the situation said its attitude might have been different if MGM's revised bid had been higher. But Vivendi considers it too low, several people familiar with the matter said.

If the five remaining bidders don't raise their offers significantly, Vivendi is likely to emphasize its willingness to go the IPO route. However, an IPO would take more time. Vivendi doesn't have a chief executive to oversee the businesses, making an IPO tough to market to investors. Hiring a CEO for the entertainment units would certainly delay the operation for several months.

The auction should drag on for several more weeks and isn't likely to be resolved until some time in August, if not later. Vivendi has asked bidders to submit proposed contract terms by the end of this month. In auctions, the contractual terms can be as important as the price offered.

Another divestiture strategy is termed a spin-off. While public firms have employed a spin-off strategy to successfully increase parent firm value, the strategy has not been fully exploited by owners of private firms. As a general rule, spin-off strategies are viable for private firms with multiple stockholders that have at least two *strategic business units* (SBUs), which are defined as self-contained businesses within the larger firm. Typically, an SBU can be split from the parent without creating any substantive operating inefficiencies within the parent. Private firms that fit this description include firms with multiple investor groups, such as professional investment firms and other supraminority investors, who believe their investment is worth more if the divisions can be valued separately.

As shown in Figure 2.4, in a spin-off a parent firm distributes shares on a pro rata basis to its stockholders. These new shares give shareholders ownership rights in a division or part of the company that is sold off. Management hopes that the value of the spun-off division will be assigned a higher value by investors than its implied value as part of the parent firm.

The use of spin-offs rather than divestitures to effectively shed assets became very popular in the 1990s. The primary motivation for this switch was the tax advantages associated with spin-offs that were no longer available if assets were sold for cash. Prior to the repeal of the General Utilities Doctrine in the 1980s, firms could sell assets without any capital gains consequences. After its repeal, spin-offs became an attractive alternative for a parent firm since shareholders received stock, not cash, and thus there were no tax consequences for the selling parent.

Although spin-offs do not produce additional cash for shareholders, they can create additional firm value. When a division is spun off, a new entity is formed with newly issued equity shares. Shareholders now own shares of the parent and shares of the spun unit. To the extent that there are potential buyers for the spun unit that were unwilling to buy the shares of the parent when the spun unit was part of the parent, a spin-off strategy creates additional liquidity for the shareholders. This additional liquidity translates into additional value.

In other cases, separating the division from the parent allows management of the division to take advantage of business opportunities that it could not as part of a larger entity, and in the process create additional value for parent firm shareholders. For example, some years back a large insurance firm spun off its money management division into a wholly owned subsidiary to enhance its competitive position in the investment management marketplace. Prior to the spin-off, all investment decisions had to be sanctioned by the insurance firm's investment policy committee, which caused unnecessary delays. In addition, because it was part of a large bureaucratic organization, customer perception was that the firm was not nimble enough to take advantage of investment opportunities as they emerged. Because of the spin-off, this

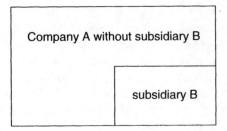

Shareholders own shares of combined company and therefore also own implied equity in the subsidiary.

(a) *Pre-Spin-Off Company*

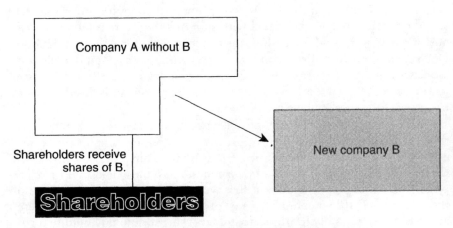

Shareholders still own shares of Company A, which now represent ownership of A without B.

(b) *Post-Spin-Off Company*

FIGURE 2.4   Spin-Off

perception quickly changed, and yet the money management subsidiary retained the cachet of being affiliated with a large, financially strong parent. Subsequent to the spin-off, the firm's performance improved relative to peer companies, and the hoped-for increase in customers and cash flow followed.

While spin-offs make sense, the real question is whether they create value. There have been a number of academic studies that indicate that spin-offs positively impact the value of the firm. Schipper and Smith report that, on average, shareholders receive an extra 2.84 percent return because of spin-offs, and this additional return increases as the spun division is a larger percentage of the parent.[5] In terms of dollar value, the value of the parent increases by the value of spun division. For example, if the value of parent prior to the spin-off is $100, and the value of the spun division is $10, then the post-spin-off value of the parent is $110.

Equity Carve-Outs

An equity carve-out is the sale of an equity interest in a subsidiary of a firm. A new legal entity is created whose shareholders may not own equity in the firm of the divesting parent. This new entity has its own management team and is run as a separate and distinct business. The parent may not necessarily retain control of the carve-out, but the divesting parent receives a cash payment that typically exceeds the implied equity value when the carve-out was part of the parent. Unlike a spin-off, an equity carve-out produces cash for the parent since it sells a percentage of the equity shares in the new firm to investors and retains the remainder. After the transaction is complete, the shareholders of the parent have reduced their ownership in the carved-out division. In contrast, a spin-off strategy leaves the parent firm shareholders with the same interest in the spun division as they had before the spin-off.

A private firm can easily accomplish an equity carve-out. While divisions of a parent are typically carved out when the parent is a public firm, because of the smaller size of private firms, divisional carve-outs would generally not be practical. However, there is no reason why a particular product line or a segment of a division could not form the basis of an equity carve-out. In this case, the private firm would form a new entity and then sell shares. Figure 2.5 shows how an equity carve-out works.

Like spin-offs, equity carve-outs have been shown to produce substantial incremental returns for investors of the parent firm. Schipper and Smith report that shareholders of parent firms that undertook equity carve-outs posted average incremental returns of 1.8 percent.[6] In short, outright sale of a division, spin-offs, and equity carve-outs are external strategies designed to unleash value that cannot be achieved under the predivestiture business organization. While public firms adopt these strategies to increase share prices, they are also viable options for private firms and offer a means to create a more valuable private entity.

THE CONTROL GAP

Figure 2.1 shows that in-place internal and external strategies are expected to produce a firm worth $3,000. However, a potential buyer may be willing

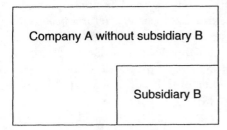

Shareholders

Shareholders implicity own 100% of equity of subsidiary B through their Company A shares.

(a) *Company before Carve-Out*

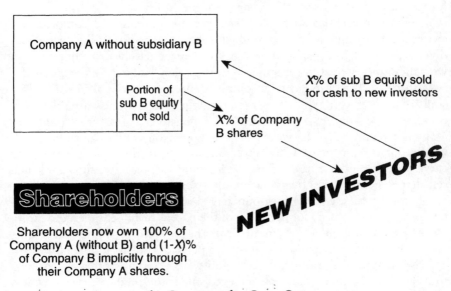

Shareholders

Shareholders now own 100% of Company A (without B) and (1-*X*)% of Company B implicitly through their Company A shares.

(b) *Company after Carve-Out*

FIGURE 2.5   Equity Carve-Out

to pay an additional sum of as much as $500 to control the firm's assets. The control gap emerges when the value of the firm to a buyer exceeds the value to the current ownership. There are two types of control buyers, each having different options but nevertheless willing to pay a premium for the target. The first type we term the *business-as-usual* (BAU) buyer. This buyer adopts the same overall strategy as the seller but brings a more professional management style to the business with the expectation of creating a more efficient operation and generating higher cash flows from the assets in place. A common example of this type of buyer is a former executive of a major public firm, typically a baby boomer, whose career has run its course in a large corporate setting and who desires to be a business owner. This former executive is considering the purchase of a private firm that he believes can benefit from his management skill with the hope of creating greater efficiencies and greater cash flow. This is the basis for his willingness to pay a premium for the business in the first place.

The second type is the strategic purchaser. This buyer believes that by combining assets of the target and the acquiring firm, additional cash flows become available that would not otherwise be possible. The strategic buyer has options, because of the assets it already owns, that the BAU buyer does not. These options potentially enable the strategic buyer to create incremental cash flows that are larger and last longer than those that a BAU buyer can be expected to create. In short, the incremental value that a strategic buyer can create will always exceed that of a BAU buyer. This leads to principle 7:

Principle 7. *A strategic buyer will always pay more for a target than a BAU buyer because the strategic buyer has more options than the BAU buyer does.*

Although there are other examples of this phenomenon, one need only refer to the FSI case to understand how a control value emerges that is larger than the value of the target with in-place strategies. Here, FPI exercised its external strategy and purchased a number of smaller financial service firms, then turned around and sold the new, larger organization to FSI, which was willing to purchase this business at a control value that exceeded what a BAU buyer would be willing to pay. The difference emerges because FSI is a strategic buyer, with options for the use of FPI's assets that would be available only to it and not to a BAU buyer.

What might these strategic options be? There are many, but one that would certainly be available is a broader array of products and services that FPI, even under a new BAU management team, could not afford to offer. Financial services firms face significant administrative and legal oversight burdens. Despite broker-dealer affiliations that have allowed smaller financial services firms to reduce administrative overhead, these costs remain significant and are becoming more so given the ever-increasing legal oversight hurdles that these firms face. In short, by integrating operations with a much larger parent, the acquirer can offer both economies of scale and scope to the target that would result in a sizable reduction in the administrative and distribution fixed costs, thereby increasing the target's profit margins well above what would be possible if the target were left to its own devices.

PRIVATE FIRM VALUE AND TRANSPARENCY

In addition to taking advantage of profit growth opportunities, the value of any firm is influenced by the quality of its financial and operational disclosures. Public firms with management that has a policy of timely disclosure of operational and financial information will always have a higher value than identical firms that do not adopt policies that encourage transparency. Transparency reduces investor uncertainty, yielding a reduced cost of capital and a higher firm value. Accurate financial reporting, ethical management behavior, and transparency come under the central rubric of *good governance*. A recent study by GovernanceMetrics indicates that firms that receive high marks on governance issues seem to be rewarded for their good behavior by the stock market, as shown in Figure 2.6.

Based on these results, one would expect that private firms that are well run and are characterized by accurate financial reporting would also be rewarded with higher values for their good behavior. Since equities of private firms do not trade on a market, the daily impact on value from good governance is not seen except on those occasions when the firm's equity needs to be valued. This occurs more frequently than one might think. For example, the positive effect of transparency will ordinarily arise when private firms are for sale and the buyers are carrying out normal due diligence, when a firm is attempting to obtain outside financing from a bank or private equity firm, and/or when a firm is providing critical financial and operational information to joint venture partners and to large public firm customers. Although the value of the firm is not calculated in each of these instances, the effect of meeting high standards of transparency does ultimately translate to higher firm value. Signs of poor record keeping, excessive compensation to family members, evidence of mixing personal and business expenses, sweetheart deals related to rental agreements, loans to owners at below market rates—all raise concern that there may be more skeletons in the closet. While these adjustments usually result in a lower tax bill, either because expenses are artificially high, as seen by mixing personal and business expenses, or because revenues are too low, a typical result of loans to shareholders at below market rates, these benefits quickly become

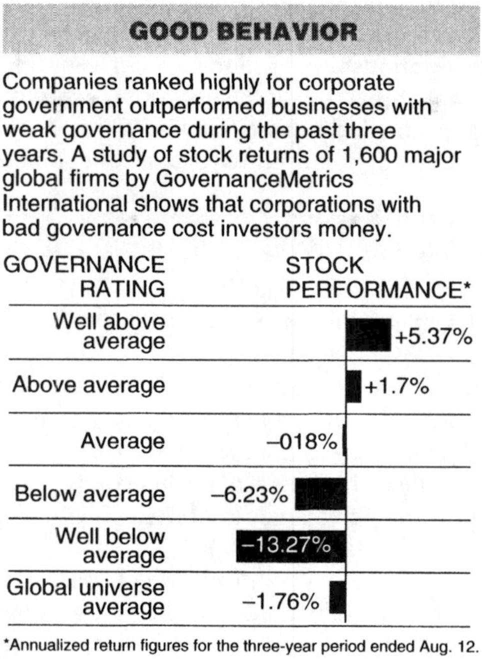

GOOD BEHAVIOR

Companies ranked highly for corporate government outperformed businesses with weak governance during the past three years. A study of stock returns of 1,600 major global firms by GovernanceMetrics International shows that corporations with bad governance cost investors money.

GOVERNANCE RATING	STOCK PERFORMANCE*
Well above average	+5.37%
Above average	+1.7%
Average	−018%
Below average	−6.23%
Well below average	−13.27%
Global universe average	−1.76%

*Annualized return figures for the three-year period ended Aug. 12.

FIGURE 2.6   Good Behavior

burdensome costs when the firm is ready to be sold. The reason is that outsiders will always accord a less transparent firm a higher risk resulting in a higher cost of capital than a firm that is more transparent. This higher cost of capital results in a firm with a lower value. Finally, having customers with a well-known reputation for dealing only with firms that meet and exceed certain credit and other performance standards means that the firm-customer relationship is "sticky," and the cash flow that emanates from it will have a longer duration and therefore be worth more, which of course translates into higher value.

While the vast majority of private firms are small, and issues of transparency typically abound, the larger a private firm is the greater the degree of transparency that is required. The reason is that a private firm's stakeholders—customers, suppliers, joint-venture partners, and creditors—have a need to understand the extent to which management/owner decisions may impact the contracting arrangements the firm has with each of its stakeholders. The information these relationships require should not be confused with the reporting requirements of public firms to accurately disclose. Rather, the type, quantity, and quality of required information arises from the need to properly assess the risks of doing business with private firms.

For example, most public firms that have private firm vendors require that these firms disclose critical financial information to them before they will enter into a vendor relationship, let alone a joint venture. It goes without saying that banks and other credit institutions keep close tabs on their private firm clients, particularly those for whom they have extended long-term debt or have made other substantive financial commitments.

PRIVATE COMPANIES ALSO FEEL PRESSURE TO CLEAN UP ACTS

By Matt Murray
Staff Reporter of the *Wall Street Journal*, July 22, 2003

The Sarbanes-Oxley Act is aimed at making publicly traded companies more accountable. But it's having a big impact on privately owned companies as well. Dick Jackson, chief financial officer of Road & Rail Services Inc., doesn't have to file public reports on his company's operations. The logistics and transportation concern, based in Louisville, Kentucky, has just three owners.

But in recent months, Road & Rail, which has 400 employees and about $25 million in annual sales, has been tweaking its corporate-governance practices. Mr. Jackson has added layers of review to the process of compiling financial results, and boosted accountability by ensuring that different managers are responsible for approving invoices and signing checks. The board is contemplating inviting one or more independent directors aboard.

Why the changes? Mr. Jackson says his company, like others, has been learning from the scandals at Enron Corp., WorldCom Inc., and elsewhere. So have a growing number of its clients—along with its banks and insurance companies—and they want to ensure Road & Rail can back up its books as well as its promises. Many of its clients are public companies that have overhauled their own governance in response to the new regulations, Mr. Jackson says.

"Philosophically, as a privately held company, you don't want everything exposed to the world," he says. "On the other hand, the world is changing, and there's a lot more sharing of information between customers and suppliers and business partners. I think everything eventually is an external event."

Indeed, the Sarbanes-Oxley Act is having a ripple effect "much more far-reaching than any of us knew," Mr. Jackson says.

Among the changes, closely held companies are quietly overhauling their boards and upgrading their accounting standards. In addition to addressing their own concerns, managers are being pressured to make changes by customers, investors, accountants, and venture capitalists. Many companies also are reacting to the rising cost of insurance for directors and officers.

Just last month, a federal judge in New York City ruled that directors at bankrupt Trace International Holdings Inc. failed in their responsibilities by allowing its chairman and controlling shareholder, Marshall Cogan, to exhaust funds through excessive compensation, dividends, and loans. The decision makes it clear that "private company directors and officers are going to be held to the same standard as public company officers and directors to determine whether or not they are fulfilling their fiduciary duties," says John P. Campo, a partner at LeBoeuf, Lamb, Greene & MacRae LLP, who represents the bankruptcy trustee in that case.

To be sure, most private companies have stopped far short of the measures adopted by their public peers, and executives at many remain tight-lipped about their operations to outsiders and even employees and some investors. After all, avoiding the spotlight and the paperwork that comes with being public is part of the reason that many stay private. "I want the right disciplines in place," says Marilyn Carlson Nelson, chairwoman and chief executive of Carlson Companies Inc. in Minneapolis, a family-controlled company that owns an array of hotel, marketing, and travel industry chains and brands, including T.G.I. Friday's restaurants and Radisson Hotels & Resorts. She adds that she doesn't want employees or investors "worried" about governance at the company, which through its own and franchised operations oversees 198,000 workers and about $20 billion in sales. But at the same time, she says, "We can't become so rigid that we lose the sense of innovation and become totally risk-averse. Our intention is to be transparent in what we do, but our intention is not to make the board into managers and operators of the company." Entrepreneurs are by nature risk takers, she says, adding, "We don't claim to the board or to each other that we're never going to fail or something won't go wrong." Of late, Carlson has been taking a more active role in monitoring external auditors and expanding internal control and disclosure requirements, such as those involving off-balance-sheet commitments, says its chief financial officer, Martyn R. Redgrave. The company's board already had independent directors and an audit committee, he notes.

"The standard I have applied is that if we find the rules relative to current practices would increase transparency or awareness, we are in favor of them," he says. But he adds that some of the new requirements are "form over substance" and says, "We're not going to sweep through our entire global system to do what is required for public companies. We're using it as a new benchmark against which we measure ourselves, and we have a lot of it in place."

Perhaps the companies most affected in the new climate are small, entrepreneurial ventures that need venture-capital funding and have high hopes of one day going public. At Celleration Inc., a tiny medical-technology company in Minneapolis with nine employees and no revenue, Chairman and CEO Kevin Nickels last year structured his six-member board so that four directors were outsiders: two of them investors and two of them industry figures. Neither of the two insiders—Mr. Nickels and company founder and chief technology officer Eliaz Babaev—sits on the audit or compensation committees.

Part of the motivation for such measures is pragmatic. "What you're doing is building the confidence for new investors," says Mr. Nickels. "You're not going to get financed unless money sources trust you."

But he says he also had a strong belief, as a manager, in the importance of independent outsiders on his board. "It's common sense," he says. "Rarely does an individual make it happen. It's usually a team of people, and a team is successful when you bring in all the bright ideas of a broadly experienced and deep group of people."

SUMMARY

This chapter outlined the various factors that determine the value of private firms, and in particular set down a number of operating principles that should guide the owners of private businesses and their advisors when they undertake any strategic initiative. The basic principle is that generating more profit from any activity does not necessarily translate to increased value unless the rate of return earned exceeds the financial cost of under-taking it. In this context, the MVM is an efficient way to ascertain whether the basic business activity an owner is contemplating undertaking makes financial sense.

CHAPTER 3

The Restructuring of Frier Manufacturing

Frier Manufacturing is a producer of components for industrial ovens and also offers industrial oven repair and maintenance services. Linking components and services appeared to make economic sense, because Frier could both sell components to industrial oven OEMs and supply them to their services subsidiary. Its major clients are restaurants and fast-food chains, with virtually all of its business located in the United States. The founders, who no longer run day-to-day operations, have a controlling interest in Frier, with the remainder of ownership split among 20 minority shareholders, several of whom have large interests and are members of the board of directors. These owners, in their early sixties, were hoping to monetize their interests in Frier through either selling their shares outright or growing the firm to the point where an IPO would be a possibility. The board of directors recently appointed Richard Fox, a major shareholder, as CEO, with the charge to develop and implement a plan that will achieve the owners' financial objectives over the next several years.

To date, the financial performance of Frier Manufacturing has been disappointing. The weak economy and a customer base that increasingly depended on OEMs, rather than third-party suppliers, for repair and maintenance services forced Frier to reduce prices to remain competitive. Profit margins suffered as a result. Since the demand for industrial ovens remained depressed, the derived demand for components was also weak, resulting in a significant drag on sales and earnings. The one bright spot was that the demand for replacement components was increasing at a healthy clip, because end users, facing a weak economy, were inclined to repair old industrial ovens rather than replace them with new equipment. Since the volume of components per order is less for replacement orders than when new ovens are produced, Frier was not reaping the economies of scale that would normally accrue when the business was driven by the demand for industrial ovens.

Although Richard Fox knew the industrial oven business very well, he was concerned about suffering from the myopia that accompanies the strategic vision of CEOs who are too close to the businesses they run. He knew he needed a brainstorming partner to help him think through the critical strategic, operational, and valuation issues that were sure to emerge as he embarked on his journey to stoke Frier's growth engine. The consulting firm Fox hired proposed to use the value circle framework as the point of departure.

INITIATING THE VALUE CIRCLE FRAMEWORK

To begin the evaluation process, the consulting firm first reviewed Frier's basic business structure. Figure 3.1 shows that Frier Manufacturing reported $20 million in revenue, a before-tax profit of $1.75 million and a before-tax profit margin of 8.75 percent. Its two strategic business units (SBUs), components and services, reported profit margins of 10 percent and 5 percent, respectively. On first pass, Fox was surprised that the margins in the service business were so low, but after further thought he realized that Frier did not have service contracts in place, and thus Frier was incurring marketing costs that its OEM competitors, for the most part, did not have to absorb. Clearly, this was an area that required further exploration, and as the analysis proceeded, it became a central focus of the consulting team. While the components business was carrying the firm, and its margins were comparable with other firms in the industry, Fox wondered whether production and perhaps distribution efficiencies were possible beyond those that had already been put in place by the previous CEO.

To understand the valuation implications of Frier's past financial performance, he asked the consulting team to value Frier's equity at the end of each month between 1998 and 2002.[1] These equity valuations were equivalent to common stock prices of public firms. Hence, Fox reasoned, and the

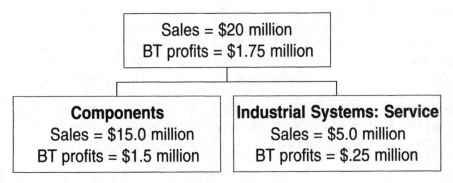

FIGURE 3.1 Financial Overview: Frier Manufacturing

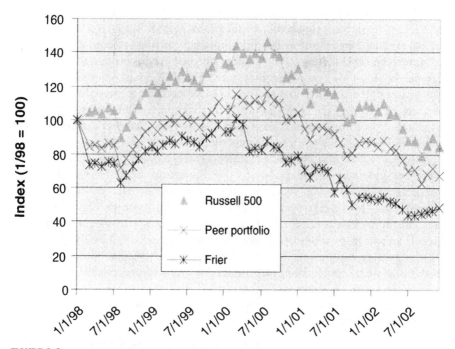

FIGURE 3.2   Comparative Stock Performance: Monthly

consulting firm concurred, that Frier's month-end equity values could be compared to both the broad stock market, measured by the performance of the Russell 5000, and a selected public firm peer group. This would answer a nagging question posed by the board: Would they have been better off investing in the public market than hoping to hit a home run by investing in Frier? Remember, these board members were owners, albeit minority shareholders, but they intuitively believed that they had made a mistake, and they wanted to know how much it cost them. Figure 3.2 shows the comparative equity analysis.

Richard Fox noted that over the past five years, Frier's equity performance lagged behind that of a portfolio of peer firms and the broader market index. These findings confirmed the worst fears of the board. Although they knew that Frier had underperformed, which was the stimulus for hiring Richard Fox in the first place, they had no idea how bad things really were. The valuation snapshots provided by their accounting firm at each year-end meeting belied the significance of the firm's poor performance.

To say the board was shocked by this analysis was an understatement. The question was how to proceed from there and, more important, how to meet the ultimate objective of monetizing their ownership. How might they get the business to a point that would make this objective a reality? The analysis made it clear to the board that reported earnings offered not only an incomplete picture of firm performance, but often a highly inaccurate one, particularly when the firm's earnings, as in Frier's case, had actually shown an increase, albeit a modest one. They became convinced that whatever the direction of earnings, if Frier's equity valuation was not increasing, Frier's performance was not only unacceptable, but worse, Frier was not on a path to meet its central objective of maximizing the value of ownership equity.

Before Richard Fox began to explore a restructuring plan, he wanted to know the valuation implications of three scenarios. The first assumed no growth and no debt. The second adopted the no-growth assumption and assumed that the assets would be financed partially with debt. The debt level determined by the consulting team analysis was the one that maximized Frier's equity value or its optimal capital structure. The third valuation scenario estimated the value of the firm if the strategic plans of Fox's predecessor were carried out and financed at the optimal capital structure. The initial results are shown in Table 3.1.

The consultant team summarized the results of their analysis and presented them to Richard Fox:

- The optimal or target capital structure for Frier Manufacturing is 78 percent equity and 22 percent debt.
- Although each business unit has some investment opportunities that can be expected to increase Frier's value above its cash cow value, in

TABLE 3.1 Cash Cow, Adjusted Cash Cow, and Going-Concern Value of Frier Manufacturing ($ Millions)

SBU	Cash Cow Value	Adjusted Cash Cow Value	Going-Concern Value: Investment and Sales Grow at Historical Rates
Components	$18.00	$26.00	$27.00
Service	$6.00	$9.00	$10.00
Total value of units	$24.00	$35.00	$37.00
Size premium*	2.50	2.50	2.50
Total firm value	$26.50	$37.50	$39.50
Mkt. value of debt	0	$8.25	$8.69
Equity value	$26.50	$29.25	$30.81

*Since Frier is larger than each SBU, it is accorded a lower cost of capital than each unit individually. This means that Frier is worth more than the aggregation of each SBU's value. The difference is the value created simply due to size.

terms of the total firm, the investment strategy outlined by Fox's predecessor adds a little less than 6 percent in value relative to Frier's adjusted cash cow value.

Richard Fox was intrigued and at the same time puzzled by the fact that historical investment rates generated such small increases in value. It was clear that the firm was earning rates of return that were only marginally greater than the firm's cost of capital, and therefore his focus turned to what could be done internally to improve the firm's cash flow prospects.

INTERNAL OPPORTUNITIES

The consultant team worked with Fox to determine how best to develop estimates for the four critical determinants of firm cash flow and their impact on the values of each of the business units. These four determinants, or value drivers, are:

1. Sales volume growth.
2. Productivity growth.
3. Change in the ratio of output price to input price.
4. Change in fixed and working capital requirements.

Sales

Sales volume increases depend on four critical factors: (1) growth of new and existing customer markets for each SBU's products and/or services, (2) sensitivity of customer demand to changing output prices (i.e., elasticity of demand), (3) changing quality standards of product/service performance, and (4) timing of introduction of new products and services.

Margin Improvements

Margins increase when productivity increases and when output prices rise relative to input prices. The relationship of both to margin improvement is shown in Equation 3.1. Increases in productivity or efficiency allow the firm to produce the same volume of goods with a lower resource base or increase volume with no increase in the level of resources. In either case, output per unit of input rises.

Determinants of the Margin Ratio

$$\text{Margin ratio} = \text{operating profits (\$)} / \text{sales (\$)}$$

$$\text{Margin ratio} = 1 - (Q_I/Q_O)(P_I/P_O)$$

(3.1)

where Q_I = weighted average input
        Q_O = weighted average output
         P_I = weighted average input price
        P_O = weighted average output price

The ratio of Q_I/Q_O is the inverse of productivity. Thus, when productivity increases, this ratio is lowered and the margin is thereby increased, all else remaining unchanged. This new margin is applied to each dollar of sales, thereby permanently raising the firm's cash flow. Again, whether firm value increases depends on the incremental capital expenditures that the productivity improvement requires. In those cases where the measured efficiency improvement is entirely the result of management deciding to downsize, the amount of additional capital required is likely to be small. Thus, to the extent such downsizing does not result in any deterioration in the benefits customers expect from the firm's products or services, this strategy will create a significant increase in firm value.

In general, however, productivity improvement requires an increase in fixed capital. Such outlays might include expenditures for redesigning a factory floor, retraining workers, implementing just-in-time inventory procedures, and updating the firm's computer systems. Feldman and Sullivan have shown that because productivity increases have a long-lasting impact on firm cash flow, investors tend to place a large value on such increments relative to the value created by other value drivers.[2]

In addition to productivity increases, margin improvements can also result from a decrease in relative prices, or the ratio of an input price index to an output price index. Since a firm uses many inputs to produce its product or service, one can think of the firm's input price as a weighted average of prices of each of the individual inputs used by the firm in its production process relative to that at a base year. For example, if 50 percent of a firm's total cost were labor and the remainder represented the purchase of metal, the firm's weighted average input price index can be approximated as $0.5 \times (1.20) + 0.5 \times (1.10) = 1.15$. The 1.15 means that the total weighted average input price is 15 percent higher than in a predetermined base year. If one assumes that the output price index for this firm is 1.30, then the ratio of 1.15 to 1.30 is the inverse of the unit price margin. In this example, the firm's unit price margin is 13 percent per unit.

Table 3.2 provides an example of how changes in productivity and relative prices are likely to impact a firm's margin. Using the formula in Equation 3.1 and base case data, Table 3.2 shows that the firm's base case margin is 20 percent. If either relative prices or the inverse of productivity decrease by 10 percent, the margin will increase by 8 percentage points above its base case value. If both increase by 10 percent, the margin increases by 15 percentage points.

TABLE 3.2   Impact of Increase in Productivity and Relative Price on a Firm's Profit Margin

Base Case: Revenues = $1,000
Total costs = $800
Output price index value = 1.30
Input price index value = 1.15
Margin = 20%

Relative Price Productivity	Base Case	10% Increase
Base case	20%	28%
10% increase	28%	35%

RESTRUCTURING FRIER MANUFACTURING

While Richard Fox was familiar with the various value-driver concepts, he was still unclear about the relationship between various strategic options and what each implied for the assumed values of the value drivers. To help management better understand the relationship between alternative strategies, the calibration of value drivers, and the value of each SBU, the consultant team performed a scenario analysis. This exercise offered insights into which of the value drivers created the most value for Frier, and what their magnitude needed to be to generate the desired effect on the value of Frier. Fox understood that, strategically, Frier needed to confront the business issue that customers were purchasing service contracts from industrial oven OEMs rather than from firms like Frier. Thus, having an OEM SBU would strategically leverage both the components and service divisions. He therefore instructed the consultant team to explore ways that would yield more cash flow from his predecessor's plan, and, in addition, he suggested to the team that they consider the option of investing internally to create an OEM manufacturer of industrial ovens. The first-stage results of this exercise are shown in Figure 3.3

The results of this analysis, shown in Table 3.1, suggest the following conclusions:

- Relative to other value drivers, margins improvements created the most value. Because Frier had little product pricing power and little leverage with its suppliers, productivity increases were the only source for these margin improvements.
- Reducing the amount of capital needed to increase output adds value to the component business, suggesting that a less capital-intensive production process would not compromise quality, and thus would not hurt future sales.

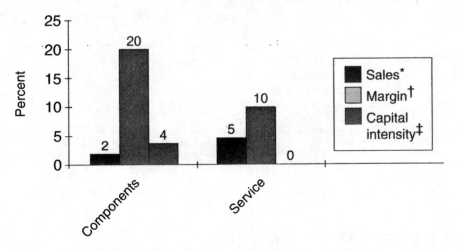

*Sales = 1% increase in sales growth.
†Margin increases by one percentage point (e.g., from 12% to 13%).
‡Capital intensity declines by 0.10 (e.g., from 0.25 times the change in sales to 0.15 times the change in sales).

FIGURE 3.3 Scenario Analysis: Percent Increase from Going-Concern Value Resulting from Changes in Value Drivers

- The service business had relatively little fixed capital requirements, although it does have working capital needs. The analysis indicated that working capital improvements would not yield any additional value indicating that Frier has reached its optimal efficiency level in this area.
- The sales volume-induced valuation increase for both SBUs was small because each dollar of sales required additional investment that did not generate a sufficient return relative to Frier's cost of financial capital.

Table 3.3 shows the valuation implications of the preceding analysis, revealing that Frier's value can be increased significantly through margin improvement. In addition, creating an industrial oven division, despite the hefty investment required, could add value to the overall operation. Richard Fox, delighted by this outcome because it validated his gut feeling about the firm's direction, was nevertheless surprised that creating an industrial oven SBU did not create additional value. The consulting team suggested that creating a business from scratch has start-up costs that buying a business in the industry would not have. The most daunting costs were those associated with creating name recognition. Surprisingly, Frier was known as a components shop; it was thought of as a low-cost provider of components, not as a high-value integrated manufacturer of industrial ovens. For Frier to earn the confidence of customers that it could deliver a high-quality, low-cost, industrial oven came at a price that Fox had not bargained for. He asked the consulting team to explore acquisition alternatives and to identify several candidates. The targets could be U.S. or foreign; however, because most of Frier's business was in the United States, an American target would be preferred (but not required).

At the time the consulting team was initiating its acquisition analysis, representatives of HP, a wholly owned industrial oven subsidiary of a large public firm, contacted Fox about a possible buyout. HP needed to expand its components business, since purchasing from contract shops like Frier was costly in terms of long delivery times as well as receiving products of poor quality that could not be used in the industrial oven production process. Having control of the upstream operations was critical to HP improving its competitive position in the marketplace. Relative to other businesses owned by its parent, HP made a small value contribution, in part because it was small relative to the other businesses owned by the parent, but more important, its management had not been successful in transforming the business into a market leader. HP's management convinced its parent that a successful acquisition strategy would allow HP to establish market dominance and thus create the value that the parent was looking for. Discussions began in earnest. As the parties began to address the terms of a sale and this information was communicated to parent management, it became clear that divesting HP was in the best interest of the parent. Fox, not totally shocked by the change of direction, realized that acquiring HP at the right price would be a good deal for Frier.

TABLE 3.3 Internal Growth Value: Frier Manufacturing ($ Millions)

	Going-Concern Value	Internal Growth Value Strategies (Sources)
Components	$27.00	$32.40 [margin]
Service	$10.00	$11.50 [sales + margin]
Industrial systems		Value created = $10.00
		Investment cost = $10.00
		Net value = $0
Total value of units	$37.00	$43.90
□ Size premium	$2.50	$3.50
Total firm value	$39.50	$47.40
Market value of debt	8.69	$10.43
Equity value	$30.81	$36.97

Before Fox moved forward on the acquisition, he needed to know whether Frier could purchase HP's subsidiary at a price that was below the cost of Frier creating the business on its own. The consulting team had determined that the investment cost to create the oven division would be $12 million, which was about equal to the value of cash flows the division was expected to create. Creating the oven division did not appear to be a wise investment. HP's parent realized that the performance of the subsidiary would never meet the financial objectives set for it by the parent; managing the operation would require a great deal of management time with very little payoff, and it would prevent management from taking advantage of other activities that would create value for the parent's shareholders. HP's management knew that Frier needed an industrial oven division as a catalyst for its other businesses, and, given this need, they believed they could extract a relatively high price for its oven business.

In the end, Frier paid $10 million for HP's industrial oven division. The present value of the expected cash flows was $12 million, so the net value created by the acquisition was $2 million. The value created by internal improvements and the acquisition resulted in Frier being worth $49.40 million.

THE FINAL DEAL STRUCTURE

The acquisition was a cash transaction and therefore taxable. Taxable acquisitions of subsidiaries can be structured in one of three ways. The structure chosen is always the one that minimizes the after-tax cost of the transaction to both the buyer and the seller. The consulting team reviewed the various options with Fox in some detail. The three basic taxable structures in which a corporation can sell a subsidiary are:

1. A taxable asset sale.
2. A taxable stock sale.
3. A taxable stock sale with a 338(h)(10) election.

In an asset sale, the net assets are transferred to the buyer, and the seller receives cash. In this case, the selling entity does not disappear, but rather its balance sheet reflects that its net assets have been exchanged for cash. In a stock sale, the acquirer purchases the stock of the target. The acquirer effectively purchases all the assets and liabilities of the target, and the target becomes a subsidiary of the acquirer post acquisition.

An acquirer and a divesting parent can structure the sale to be a stock sale while treating the transaction as an asset sale for tax purposes. Section 338(h)(10) provides a way to retain the favorable tax treatment of an asset sale without incurring the nontax costs of an asset sale. Under 338(h)(10), a sale of subsidiary stock can be taxed as an asset sale if both the buyer and seller agree to structure the transaction in this way. In a qualifying stock purchase with at least 80 percent of the target's stock obtained during a 12-month period, the divesting parent and the acquirer can jointly make a 338(h)(10) election. The taxable gain or loss on the transaction is calculated as the acquisition price less the divesting parent's basis in the net assets of the target. No tax is assessed on the difference between the purchase price and the divesting parent's book value basis in the stock.

The consultant team advised Fox that an asset transaction rather than a stock transaction was preferred and a 338(h)(10) was not optimal. There are two advantages to an asset sale. The first relates to the present value of tax benefits that result from enhanced depreciation and amortization write-offs. These emerge because the lower book value of purchased assets on the seller's balance sheet can now be stepped up to their fair market value on the acquirer's balance sheet, and depreciation and amortization schedules can now be applied to these higher values. Second, by purchasing assets rather than stock, the acquirer is not liable for past transgressions of the target's management that might emerge during the postacquisition period and that due diligence could never be expected to identify, let alone value. An asset sale severs the legal connection between the buyer and seller, whereas a stock sale does not.

In contrast, a 338(h)(10) election preserves the former advantage of an asset purchase, but not the latter. Generally, a 338(h)(10) election will be demanded by the seller when the seller's basis in stock exceeds its basis in the net assets of the divested entity. This typically occurs when the divested subsidiary was not developed organically but was developed and expanded after it was acquired. In cases where the divesting parent internally generates a subsidiary, as was the case with HP, the seller is typically indifferent about how the deal is structured.

The deal was finalized as an asset transaction. Frier paid $10 million for HP's subsidiary. Frier purchased both tangible and intangible assets. Purchased tangible assets included equipment, material inventory, and receivables. Frier leased HP's manufacturing plant. Intangibles included patents, trade name, and HP's customer list.

THE CONTROL VALUE

Richard Fox was very successful in integrating HP into Frier's operations. Frier's cash flow grew at a rapid rate, and the hoped-for economies of scale in the component business emerged when management aligned the production needs of the industrial oven division with component production schedules. In addition, cash flow from Frier's industrial oven service business began to grow rapidly, since Frier was now an OEM. Two years after the acquisition, Fox engaged a consulting firm to determine whether a larger firm would have some interest in purchasing a restructured Frier. Frier's financials had not only shown marked improvement since the acquisition of the HP subsidiary, but the firm's cash flow was far more certain. In short, the valuation-creation strategy employed by Frier set the stage for the ultimate liquidity event that the board and the other owners were hoping for when Fox was appointed CEO.

The size of the control gap depends on three critical factors. The first is the nature of the buyer, as noted earlier in this chapter. The second is the competitive atmosphere of the buyout market. The third is the amount of liquidity available in the marketplace. During the mid-1980s and for most of the 1990s, each of the factors contributed to a thriving mergers and acquisitions (M&A) market. At the turn of the twenty-first century, these factors were not nearly as positive, as both a weak domestic economy and a high-risk global economic and political environment reduced the willingness of investors, particularly angel investors, private equity groups, and venture capitalists, from committing capital. This unwillingness spilled over to the established private business transaction market and influenced both the demand and the timing of the interest in Frier. However, in late 2002, several European firms expressed an interest in acquiring Frier. They each wanted a larger share of the U.S. market, and while several had a U.S. presence, they were not leading competitors to Frier in the U.S. market. After in-depth discussions with several potential acquirers, the consulting team suggested that Frier request all interested parties to submit closed bids by a fixed date. Frier would then negotiate with the winning bidder. The winner was willing to pay Frier a 30 percent premium above its fair market value. In large measure, this premium reflected the obvious synergies between the acquirer and Frier. The deal closed on March 30, 2003.

CHAPTER 4

Valuation Models and Metrics

Discounted Free Cash Flow and the Method of Multiples

In the two previous chapters we showed that the expected success of any business strategy can be evaluated based on whether it creates additional value for the owners of the firm. That said, the natural next questions are, how is created value measured, and, of the several valuation approaches that can be used, which is the most accurate? The IRS, for example, has sanctioned a number of valuation methods:

- *The asset approach.* This method first identifies a firm's tangible and intangible assets and values. The sum of these values is then equated to the value of the firm.
- *Income-based methods.* These methods project a firm's cash flow for valuation purposes over some period, discount these values to the present, and then sum these present values to obtain the value of the firm.
- *The method of multiples.* This method first identifies a set of firms that are comparable to the firm being valued. For each comparable firm, the ratio of its market price to revenue or earnings is calculated.[1] These ratios are averaged, and/or the median value is determined. The value of the target firm is then equal to the average or median revenue (earnings) multiple multiplied by the target firm's revenue (earnings).

As a theoretical matter, value should be independent of the valuation model used. As a practical matter, this is generally not the case. The reason is that the inputs that each method requires may not be consistent across valuation approaches, and hence a different answer emerges depending on which method is being used. For example, the income approach may indicate the firm is worth $1,000, and the method of multiples might indicate that firms like the target sell for three times revenue for a value of $1,200.

The reasons for this discrepancy are that the input values embedded in the comparable revenue multiple of 3 are different than the input values used in the income approach. Valuation analysts understand that the information required by each valuation model are not necessarily consistent and therefore accept the fact, with some limitation, that each valuation method will yield a different result. Alternatively, they also recognize that multiple valuations arising out of using different valuation approaches contain relevant and important information related to the underlying value of the firm. To cope with the inconsistencies and yet retain relevant information embedded in these different values, valuation analysts weight each value to create what is in essence an expected value of the target private firm. The weights represent an analyst's judgment about the "information quotient" embedded in each valuation approach, and to this extent, the weighting is strictly subjective.

This discussion raises an interesting question: Can one do better than simply use a subjective weighted average? Put differently, is there research that indicates, for example, which valuation model is likely to produce the smallest error? To this end, this chapter compares the two most commonly used valuation approaches—*discounted free cash flow* and the *method of multiples*. The latter approach is often used because it is simple to apply. The discounted cash flow approach is more complex because it requires information on a number of factors, including, the firm's true cash flow for valuation purposes, its cost of capital, its investment requirements, and the likely growth in revenue and profits. While these values are often difficult to calculate for public firms, they are far more difficult to estimate for private firms. Before addressing the issue of which valuation model is more accurate, this chapter first defines cash flow for valuation purposes and how to construct this concept from the financials of a private firm. It then goes on to derive the discounted free cash flow method, compares it to the method of multiples, and then reviews research that indicates that the valuation error is likely to be smaller using discounted free cash flow than using the method of multiples.

DEFINING CASH FLOW FOR VALUATION PURPOSES

To calculate a firm's cash flow for valuation purposes, we use the example of Tentex. Tentex, located in the Midwest United States, is a private firm operating in the packaging machinery industry, North American Industry Classification System (NAICS)-333993, or SIC 3565. This U.S. industry comprises establishments primarily engaged in manufacturing packaging machinery, such as wrapping, bottling, canning, and labeling machinery. This sector also includes the following activities:

- Bag opening, filling, and closing machines manufacturing.
- Bread wrapping machines manufacturing.
- Capping, sealing, and lidding packaging machinery manufacturing.

- Carton filling machinery manufacturing.
- Coding, dating, and imprinting packaging machinery manufacturing.
- Food packaging machinery manufacturing.
- Labeling (i.e., packaging) machinery manufacturing.
- Packaging machinery manufacturing.
- Testing, weighing, inspecting, and packaging machinery manufacturing.
- Thermoform, blister, and skin packaging machinery manufacturing.
- Wrapping (i.e., packaging) machinery manufacturing.

Tentex specializes in designing and manufacturing low- to moderate-volume machines that provide their customers with high-quality and cost-effective solutions through the innovative use of sensors, motion controls, and other technologies. Over the past several years, Tentex has developed a strong and a growing relationship with leading packaging companies. Tentex has become the outsourced designer and manufacturer of many of the machines that are either given or rented to customers for use in the customers' packing facilities. For example, a major Internet retailer is a client of one of Tentex's partners. The partner provides the retailer with Tentex machines to use with packaging materials purchased from the Tentex partner.

To arrive at cash flow for valuation purposes, several sets of adjustments to Tentex's reported income statement need to be made. To demonstrate these adjustments, we first start with Table 4.1, which shows Tentex's income statement for 2003. The column labeled Reported Value shows that Tentex reported no profit in 2003. However, after making a series of adjustments, Tentex had a pretax profit of $640,868. Total cash flow to owners and creditors before tax is the sum of reported pretax profit plus interest expense of $55,800, or a pretax total of $696,667.82. These adjustments are of two general types. The first is related to compensation of officers and other personnel related to the owners. The second relates to discretionary expenses, or expenses that were not necessary to the business.

Compensation of Officers and Employee Family Members and Friends

Reported compensation per owner/officer is $340,760. This compensation is divided into two components. The first component is a wage, and the second component is equivalent to a dividend each owner receives. To properly account for the true cost of labor, we need to determine the market wage (including benefits) that the firm would need to pay to obtain the same services each owner currently provides. Compensation less the market wage (including benefits) equals the dividend each owner receives.

Table 4.1 shows the benchmark wage for each owner. This benchmark

TABLE 4.1 Tentex Income Statement (2003) and Compensation and Discretionary Expense Benchmarks

Row	Concepts	Reported Value	Benchmark Value	Adjustment to Earnings	Adjusted Values
1	Gross receipts less returns and allowances	$3,562,556.00	—	—	$3,562,556.00
2	Cost of goods sold	$2,030,036.00	—	—	$2,030,036.00
3	Depreciation	$250,000.00			$250,000.00
4	Compensation of officers	$681,520.00	$258,574.00	($422,946.00)	$258,574.00
	Compensation of officer 1	$340,760.00	$129,287.00	($211,473.00)	$129,287.00
	Compensation of officer 2	$340,760.00	$129,287.00	($211,473.00)	$129,287.00
5	Salaries and wages	$350,000.00	$268,810.00	($81,190.00)	$268,810.00
	Bookkeeping clerk (wife)	$50,000	$28,650.00	($21,350.00)	$28,650.00
	Secretary (son)	$45,000	$26,390.00	($18,610.00)	$26,390.00
	Product promoter (brother)	$55,000	$25,360.00	($29,640.00)	$25,360.00
	Machinist (daughter)	$45,000	$33,410.00	($11,590.00)	$33,410.00
6	Repairs and maintenance	$1,800.00	—	—	$1,800.00
7	Rents	$18,400.00	—	—	$18,400.00
8	Interest	$55,800.00	—	—	$55,800.00
9	Other deductions	$175,000.00	$38,268.38	($136,731.62)	$38,268.38
	Travel expenses	$75,000	$22,045.10	($52,954.90)	$22,045.10
	■ Family vacation	$25,000	—	—	—
	■ Trip to Super Bowl	$10,000	—	—	—
	■ Family automobile	$35,000	—	—	—
	■ Fuel for family vehicles	$5,000	—	—	—
	Entertainment expenses	$45,000	$2,622.04	($42,377.96)	$2,622.04
	■ Company parties	$20,000	—	—	—
	■ Televisions	$15,000	—	—	—
	■ Season tickets to sports teams	$10,000	—	—	—

Meals expenses	$50,000	$10,652.04	($39,347.96)	$10,652.04
■ Family dinners	$35,000	—	—	—
■ Sales dinners	$15,000	—	—	—
Club expenses	$5,000	$2,949.20	($2,050.80)	$2,949.20
Taxable income	$0.00	—	—	$640,867.62

10

Benchmark Values for NAICS for Officer Compensation

Asset size	$100,000	$500,000	$1,000,000	$5,000,000	$25,000,000	$250,000,000
National	$59,870	$97,870	$133,818	$133,818	$182,970	$299,103
Illinois	$57,843	$94,556	$129,287	$129,287	$176,774	$288,974

Src: Axiom Valuation Solutions Compensation Database

Benchmark Values for NAICS for Discretionary Expenses

Expense	Expense Benchmark (as percentage of total revenue)
Travel expense	0.6188%
Entertainment expense	0.0736%
Meals expense	0.2990%
Club fee expense	0.0828%

Src: Axiom Valuation Solutions Discretionary Expense Database

Benchmark Value from Bureau of Labor Statistics for Worker Compensation

Occupation	Value
Bookkeeping clerk	$28,650.00
Secretary	$26,390.00
Product promoters	$25,360.00
Machinist	$33,410.00

Src: Bureau of Labor Statistics

is based on the firm's industry, asset size class, and location. Tentex's asset size, located in Illinois, is $5.0 million. The benchmark wage for each owner is $129,287. The difference between compensation paid per owner and this benchmark wage is $211,473. This dividend is added back to reported pre-tax profits. The total added back from this source is $422,946.

The same adjustment for owners is made for employee family members. It is not uncommon for owners to compensate family members in excess of what the firm would have to pay if it hired equivalently skilled third parties to do the same job. Like CEO wages, occupation wage levels vary by industry and geography. Based on data from the Bureau of Labor Statistics, Tentex pays family members close to twice their market wage. Based on these adjustments, pretax profits increase by $81,190.

Discretionary Expenses

Discretionary expenses are expenses incurred that are not necessary for the normal functioning of the business. Axiom Valuation Solutions has developed a database of discretionary expense percentages by industry. The raw data is from the Department of Commerce. Axiom has taken this information and has developed discretionary expense ratios by industry. The lower part of Table 4.1 shows the ratios applicable to Tentex. By multiplying each discretionary expense ratio by Tentex's total revenue, a discretionary expense benchmark is obtained. These benchmark values are then compared to actual discretionary expenses. If the actual expenditure exceeds its benchmark, costs are reduced by the amount of the difference, and pretax profits are correspondingly increased. In cases where the firm does not spend enough in a particular category, the expense level is raised and adjusted profits would decline. In some cases, the benchmark may not be appropriate. The analyst should be cautious about adjusting the reported benchmark in these cases. At a minimum, criteria should be developed based on hard data that offers guidance about the extent to which the reported benchmark should be adjusted.

In some cases, valuation analysts refer to industry benchmark values for officers' compensation published by the Risk Management Association (RMA) in its *Annual Statement Studies*[2] rather than following the method suggested here. Member banks provide survey information on about 15,000 firms each year across a large number of industries. RMA aggregates the data by industry and size and publishes what amounts to common-size income statements and balance sheets. For example, for most industries RMA publishes officer compensation as a percentage of revenue. When using the RMA data, the valuation analyst would multiply the RMA benchmark compensation ratio by the target firm's revenue to obtain a benchmark compensation value. The difference between this value and the reported compensation would be treated as excess compensation. If this difference is positive (negative), it would imply that officer's compensation should be adjusted downward (upward).

This approach tends to understate the portion of total compensation that should be treated as a dividend if the compensation data of the sample RMA firms includes bonuses. One could argue that a bonus is required to get the right people to run the firm and therefore it is a real cost of doing business. However, what happens if the firm performs poorly and funds are not available to pay the bonus? The answer is that no bonus is paid. A wage, by comparison, reflects an implicit contract between the firm and the employee. Therefore, the firm either pays the wage or terminates the employee. The bonus is a discretionary payment that is part of the return on capital and therefore like other payments to capital should be capitalized. This suggests that using the RMA officer's compensation benchmark to adjust reported officer compensation expense will likely result in the firm being undervalued.

Further Adjustments to Arrive at Cash Flow for Valuation Purposes

Once the financial statement of the private firm is unraveled, several additional adjustments need to be made to arrive at an accurate measure of firm profit, or net operating profit after tax (NOPAT). The lower section of Table 4.2 shows how NOPAT is calculated.

To move from pretax profit to NOPAT, the former must be reduced by taxes as shown on the income statement, which in this case amounts to 40 percent of pretax profits. This after-tax result is further reduced by the interest tax shield, or the tax savings that emerges because interest is a tax-deductible expense. This adjustment is made to reflect the true tax burden on the firm's assets, which is independent of how the assets are financed.[3]

Calculating Free Cash Flow to the Firm

Free cash flow to the firm is income available to shareholders and creditors after capital requirements are accounted for. It is equal to NOPAT plus interest expense, income available to shareholders and creditors, less the sum of net capital expenditure and the change in working capital adjusted for excess cash.[4] Table 4.3 shows the relationship between NOPAT and free cash flow to the firm.

Free cash flow to the firm is equal to $275,227. This is equal to NOPAT, $362,201, less the change in working capital, $69,783, less the change in net fixed capital, $17,192. Notice that depreciation is not added back in this calculation. The reason is that adding back depreciation to income available to shareholders and creditors is offset by subtracting

TABLE 4.2 Tentex Income Statement (2003) and Calculation of NOPAT

Row	Concepts	Reported Value	Benchmark Value	Adjustment to Earnings	Adjusted Values
1	Gross receipts less returns and allowances	$3,562,556.00	—	—	$3,562,556.00
2	Cost of goods sold	$2,030,036.00	—	—	$2,030,036.00
3	Depreciation	$250,000.00			$250,000.00
4	Compensation of officers	$681,520.00	$258,574.00	($422,946.00)	$258,574.00
	Compensation of officer 1	$340,760.00	$129,287.00	($211,473.00)	$129,287.00
	Compensation of officer 2	$340,760.00	$129,287.00	($211,473.00)	$129,287.00
5	Salaries and wages	$350,000.00	$268,810.00	($81,190.00)	$268,810.00
	Bookkeeping clerk (wife)	$50,000	$28,650.00	($21,350.00)	$28,650.00
	Secretary (son)	$45,000	$26,390.00	($18,610.00)	$26,390.00
	Product promoter (brother)	$55,000	$25,360.00	($29,640.00)	$25,360.00
	Machinist (daughter)	$45,000	$33,410.00	($11,590.00)	$33,410.00
6	Repairs and maintenance	$1,800.00	—	—	$1,800.00
7	Rents	$18,400.00	—	—	$18,400.00
8	Interest	$55,800.00	—	—	$55,800.00

9	Other deductions	$175,000.00	$38,268.38	($136,731.62)	$38,268.38
	Travel expenses	$75,000	$22,045.10	($52,954.90)	$22,045.10
	▪ Family vacation	$25,000	—	—	—
	▪ Trip to Super Bowl	$10,000	—	—	—
	▪ Family automobile	$35,000	—	—	—
	▪ Fuel for family vehicles	$5,000	—	—	—
	Entertainment expenses	$45,000	$2,622.04	($42,377.96)	$2,622.04
	▪ Company parties	$20,000	—	—	—
	▪ Televisions	$15,000	—	—	—
	▪ Season tickets to sports teams	$10,000	—	—	—
	Meals expenses	$50,000	$10,652.04	($39,347.96)	$10,652.04
	▪ Family dinners	$35,000	—	—	—
	▪ Sales dinners	$15,000	—	—	—
	Club expenses	$5,000	$2,949.20	($2,050.80)	$2,949.20
10	Taxable income	$0.00			$640,867.62
11	Tax burden				
12	▪ Taxes @ 40% (Row 10 × 0.4)				$256,347.05
13	▪ Tax shield on interest (row 8 × 0.4)				$22,320.00
14	NOPAT				$362,200.57

TABLE 4.3 Tentex Balance Sheet and Calculation of Free Cash Flow

Row	Concepts	2003	2002	Change: 2003/2002
	Assets			
1	Cash	$220,000	$187,000	
2	Cash required for operations	$71,251	$64,126	
3	Excess cash	$148,749	$122,874	
4	Accounts receivable	$356,256	$302,817	
5	Inventories	$890,639	$846,107	
6	Other current assets	$0	$0	
7	Total current assets	$1,686,895	$1,522,924	
8	Gross plant and equipment	$5,343,834	$5,076,642	
9	Accumulated depreciation	$3,730,729	$3,480,729	
10	Net fixed capital	$1,613,105	$1,595,914	
11	Total assets	$3,300,000	$3,118,838	
12	**Liabilities and equity**			
13	Short-term debt and current portion of long-term debt	$200,000	$190,000	

Row	Item				
14	Accounts payable	$178,128		$160,315	
15	Accrued liabilities	$50,000		$42,500	
16	Total current liabilities	$428,128		$392,815	
17	Long-term debt	$490,000		$454,151	
18	Other long-term liabilities	$0		$90,000	
19	Deferred income taxes	$0			
20	Total shareholder equity	$2,381,872		$2,181,872	
21	Total liabilities and equity	$3,300,000		$3,118,838	
22	Working capital	$890,018	$0	$820,235	$69,783
23	Net fixed capital	$1,613,105	$0	$1,595,914	$17,192
24	Net capital requirements	$362,201			$86,974
25	NOPAT	$275,227			
26	Free cash flow to the firm (row 25–row 24)				

gross capital expenditures, which is defined as net capital expenditures plus depreciation.[5] Thus, depreciation is canceled out in the calculation of free cash flow to the firm.

Now that we know how to make the necessary adjustments to the financial statements of a private firm and in addition combine the adjusted income statement with the balance sheet to calculate free cash flow, we turn to the issue of valuing these cash flows. First, however, we review the cash flow valuation framework.

THE GENERAL VALUATION FRAMEWORK

The value of an ongoing business is related to the cash flow a buyer expects to receive from owning it. The buyer of the business expects the cash flows over time, and the size and timing of the cash flows, to be subject to a degree of uncertainty or risk. Therefore, for a business to be valued properly, the analyst needs to consider each of these factors. Finance theory tells us that if each of the valuation factors have been computed, then the value of a firm today should be equal to the sum of the present value of expected cash flow payments over the life of the asset, as shown in Equation 4.1.

$$V_0 = \frac{\hat{C}_1}{1+k} + \frac{\hat{C}_2}{(1+k)^2} + \ldots + \frac{\hat{C}_N}{(1+k)^N} \tag{4.1}$$

where V_0 = value

$\hat{C}_1 \ldots \hat{C}_N$ = expected value of free cash flow for future periods $1 - N$

k = the current discount rate

Predicting a firm's future cash flows is difficult to do with any degree of accuracy. Nevertheless, it may be possible to project the average growth rate in cash flow over an extended period of time with somewhat more accuracy. Equations 4.2 through 4.5 show the implications of imposing a constant cash flow growth on the general valuation model.

$$V_0 = \frac{C_0[1+\hat{g}]}{(1+k)} + \frac{C_0[1+\hat{g}]^2}{(1+k)^2} + \ldots + \frac{C_0[1+\hat{g}]^N}{(1+k)^N} \tag{4.2}$$

where $\hat{g}$ = the expected average annual growth rate of C and C_1 is equal to $C_0[1+\hat{g}]$

C_0 is the last cash payment received

If we define $(1+\hat{g})/(1+k)$ as λ, then V_0 is equal to $C_0\lambda[1 + \lambda + \lambda^2 + \ldots + \lambda^{N-1}]$.

If we assume that $(1+\hat{g})$ always exceeds $(1+k)$, the growth in C is greater than the discount rate k, then λ will be less than 1. If the life of the asset is long, N approaches infinity, then the term in brackets is the sum of a geometric series, which is equal to $1/(1 - \lambda)$.

$$V_0 = (C_0\lambda) \times \frac{1}{(1 - \lambda)} \quad \text{or} \quad V_0 = \frac{C_0[1 + \hat{g}]}{(k - \hat{g})} \qquad (4.3)$$

This relationship is known as the *Gordon-Shapiro constant growth model*. Using this model, we now show that a firm's multiple is directly related to the present value of a firm's cash flow.

If we assume for a moment that the asset's value is equal to its market price, P_0, and the cash payment is defined as firm net income or traditional earnings, then the Gordon-Shapiro model yields the firm's price-earnings ratio.

$$\frac{P_0}{C_0} = \frac{[1 + \hat{g}]}{(k - \hat{g})} \qquad (4.4)$$

The price-earnings multiple is an often-quoted valuation metric. To see how this multiple can be used to value the equity of a target firm, consider the following example. Let us assume that Firm A is a private firm whose shares have just been purchased for $20 per share, and earnings per share is $2. Hence, its price-earnings multiple is 10. Firm B is a private firm that is comparable to Firm A. If Firm B is currently earning $1 per share, then the value of Firm B's equity, if it were publicly traded, would be $10, or the per-share earnings of $1 times the price-earnings multiple of 10. If we assume that Firm B has 1,000 shares outstanding and $5,000 in debt, the value of the firm would be $15,000 ($10/share × 1,000 shares plus debt of $5,000).

The price-earnings multiple is also directly related to the price-revenue multiple. To see this, assume that C_0 is equal to the current cash flow profit margin, m_0, multiplied by the most recent 12 months of revenue, R_0. Substituting $m_0 \times R_0$ for C_0 yields the revenue multiple P_0/R_0.

$$\frac{P_0}{R_0} = m_0 \times \frac{[1 + \hat{g}]}{(k - \hat{g})} \qquad (4.5)$$

Note that the revenue multiple and the earnings multiple are a function of k, $\hat{g}$, and m_0. Thus two firms can be considered comparable if the values of these parameters are the same. Moreover, the value obtained for the target firm when applying the general valuation model directly, Equation 4.1, is likely to yield a different valuation result than the comparable method if the values k, $\hat{g}$, and m_0, implied by the general valuation model, are not consistent with the values of these parameters embedded in the multiples of the comparable firms. As a general rule, these parameters are rarely the same, and differences in value emerge because of this. We demonstrate this result in a subsequent section. However, first we introduce the nonconstant growth valuation model.

The Nonconstant Growth Valuation Model

The Gordon-Shapiro model can be made less restrictive by allowing cash flow growth rates over a finite time frame to vary from year to year and then assume that growth is constant from the end of the finite time frame forward. Imposing these assumptions on the general valuation equations yields Equation 4.6, the nonconstant growth model.

$$V_0 = \frac{\hat{C}_1}{1+k} + \frac{\hat{C}_2}{(1+k)^2} + \frac{\hat{C}_{n-1}}{(1+k)^n} + \ldots + \left(\frac{\hat{C}_{n-1}}{k-g}\right) \times \frac{1+g}{(1+k)^n} \quad (4.6)$$

The finite time frame between 1 and $n - 1$ is known as the *competitive advantage period*. It reflects a condition under which the firm earns a rate of return that exceeds its cost of capital. This condition is not expected to last forever, since earning monopoly rents will attract competitors that will bid down returns. As returns are bid lower, new investment opportunities with returns exceeding the cost of capital diminish. As a result, optimal use of internal funds requires that less of a firm's cash flow is used to finance new investment opportunities and more is returned to business owners in the form of dividends and distributions. As less of the firm's cash flow is used to finance new investment, the growth in future cash flows is lower as a result.

To see this consider the basic relationship between a firm's reinvestment rate, RR, rate of return on assets, ROA, and future growth in cash flows, g, as shown in Equation 4.7.

$$g_t = \text{ROA}_t \times \text{RR}_t \quad (4.7)$$

Now Equation 4.6 can be written as Equation 4.8:

$$V_0 = \text{CF}_0 \times \frac{(1 + \hat{\text{ROA}}_1 \times \text{RR}_1)}{(1+k)^1} = \frac{\hat{\text{CF}}_1}{(1+k)^1} + \hat{\text{CF}}_1 \times \frac{(1 + \hat{\text{ROA}}_2 \times \text{RR}_2)}{(1+k)^2}$$

$$= \frac{\hat{\text{CF}}_2}{(1+k)^2} + \ldots + \hat{\text{CF}}_{n-1} \times \frac{(1 + \hat{\text{ROA}}_n \times \text{RR}_n)}{(1+k)^n} = \frac{\left(\dfrac{\hat{\text{CF}}_n}{k-g}\right)}{(1+k)^n} \quad (4.8)$$

$$= V_0 = \text{CF}_0 \times [(1+\hat{g}_1)]/(1+k)^1 + [(1+\hat{g}_1) \times (1+\hat{g}_2)]/(1+k)^2$$

$$+ \ldots + \frac{[(1+\hat{g}_1) \times (1+\hat{g}_2) \times \ldots \times (1+\hat{g}_n)]}{(1+k)^n}$$

As the rate of return declines due to competitive pressures, the growth in cash flows will also decline. However, as long as ROA is greater than k, the retention rate should be large enough to fund investment requirements. In cases where investment requirements are less-than-expected after-tax cash flows, the retention rate is less than unity. When investment requirements exceed after-tax cash flows, then the firm needs outside funding in the form of new equity and/or debt. When competitive pressure results in a rate of return that equals the cost of capital, g will be zero because the retention will be zero. Put differently, reinvesting firm capital when the ROA equals k results in no additional value created by the investments made. When the long-run value of g is greater than zero, the firm has a sustainable competitive advantage, allowing it to earn rates of return that exceed the cost of capital in perpetuity.[6] Imposing competitive market conditions in Equation 4.8 implies that $\hat{g}_1 > \hat{g}_2 > \hat{g}_3 < \ldots > \hat{g}_n$, $\hat{g}_n = 0$ when $k = \text{ROA}$, and $\text{RR}_n = 0$. Thus, Equation 4.8 can be written as Equation 4.9.

$$V_0 = \hat{\text{CF}}_1/(1 + k)^1 + \hat{\text{CF}}_2/(1 + k)^2$$
$$+ \ldots + [\hat{\text{CF}}_{n-1} \times (1 + \hat{g}_n)](k - \hat{g}_n)/(1 + k)^n \qquad (4.9)$$
$$\hat{g}_n = 0 \text{ if } k = \text{ROA}$$

Based on this discussion, one might ask: Is there an optimal value for g? While there is no optimal value per se, there is a plausible range. To start, the U.S. economy has a long-term growth rate of about 5 percent (3 percent real growth and 2 percent inflation). The long-term growth in firm cash flows should not be expected to grow significantly faster than the long-term growth potential of the U.S. economy. If this were assumed, it would imply that the firm would represent an increasing share of the total economy over time, and at some point in the future the firm would be equal in size to the total economy. This implication, of course, makes no sense, and hence the long-term value of g should reflect both the long-term competitive conditions facing the firm and the long-term growth potential of the total economy. This suggests that long-term growth rates in excess of the long-term growth of the economy are not sensible.

Valuing Tentex Using the Discounted Free Cash Flow Model

In this section we use the nonconstant growth model to value Tentex. The version of the model used combines Tentex's expected cash flow with its expected capital requirements to generate what is termed *free cash flow.* More precisely, free cash flow is defined as NOPAT less the change in working capital and net capital expenditures. Table 4.4 shows the inputs used in the Tentex valuation. Table 4.5 shows the Tentex valuation and the various components that make it up.

Note that Tentex revenue is expected to grow at 7 percent a year for each of the next four years and then to slow as expansion opportunities diminish. Revenue growth is a function of two factors. They are the expected revenue growth of the packaging equipment industry and Tentex management's ability to execute its strategy. Tentex is not a national player but does service a large market area centered in the Midwest. Thus, expected Tentex's revenue growth reflects both the expected national growth of the industry and the expected nominal economic growth of Tentex's service territory.[7]

Growth in taxable income reflects management's intention to consistently increase the efficiency of its manufacturing and distribution operations. Thus, growth in taxable income is expected to exceed growth in revenue. Tentex has debt outstanding of $679,039, which will increase as it finances part of its future capital additions with debt. Interest expense will remain constant, however, since management will adjust maturities of new debt in response to expected rate changes. As rates rise, management will seek out lower rates by issuing shorter-dated debt, and it will do the opposite when rates fall. Net fixed and working capital increase at the same rate as revenue, as suggested by the multiplier theory of investment.[8] Changes in net fixed capital and working capital are equivalent to net capital expenditures and change in working capital, respectively. These values are subtracted from cash flow to shareholders and creditors to obtain free cash flow. Tentex's cost of capital is 12 percent. In Chapter 5, we show how the cost of capital is calculated. For the moment, think of this rate as a blend of

TABLE 4.4   Data Inputs Used to Value Tentex

Inputs	Values	Source
Depreciation and		
amortization growth rate	3.00%	Growth in revenue
Net fixed assets:		
Starting value	$1,613,105.00	Balance sheet
Revenue growth	7.00%	Based on industry growth factors
Net working capital:		
Starting value	$890,018.00	Balance sheet
Cost of capital	12.00%	Calculated
ROA in perpetuity	15.00%	Based on analysis of long-term competitive factors
Retention rate	20.00%	Based on investments that have returns in excess of 12%
Long-term growth	3.00%	Based on analysis of long-term competitive factors
Tax rate	40.00%	Statutory rate
Initial debt level	$490,000.00	Balance sheet

TABLE 4.5 Valuing Tentex Using the Discounted Free Cash Flow Model

Time Period	0	1	2	3	4	5	6	Value in Perpetuity
Revenue	$3,562,556	$3,811,935	$4,078,770	$4,364,284	$4,669,784	$4,809,878	$4,954,174	
Revenue growth		7.00%	7.00%	7.00%	7.00%	3.00%	3.00%	
Taxable income growth:								
Competitive advantage period		21%	10.00%	15.00%	10.00%	6.00%	5.00%	
Taxable income	$640,868	$774,051	$851,456	$979,175	$1,077,092	$1,141,718	$1,198,804	
Interest expense	$0	$55,800	$55,800	$55,800	$55,800	$55,800	$55,800	
Tax @ 40%	$256,347	$309,621	$340,583	$391,670	$430,837	$456,687	$479,522	
Tax shield on interest	$0	$22,320	$22,320	$22,320	$22,320	$22,320	$22,320	
Tax burden	$256,347	$331,941	$362,903	$413,990	$453,157	$479,007	$501,842	
NOPAT	$384,521	$442,111	$488,554	$565,185	$623,935	$662,711	$696,962	
Growth in NOPAT		15%	11%	16%	10%	6%	5%	
Cash flow to owners and creditors after tax		$442,111	$488,554	$565,185	$623,936	$662,711	$696,962	
Net fixed capital	$1,613,105	$1,726,022	$1,846,844	$1,976,123	$2,114,452	$2,177,885	$2,243,222	
Net capital expenditure		$112,917	$120,822	$129,279	$138,329	$63,434	$65,337	
Net working capital	$890,018	$1,074,979	$1,182,477	$1,359,848	$1,495,833	$1,585,583	$1,664,862	
Change in working capital		$184,961	$107,498	$177,372	$135,985	$89,750	$79,279	
Free cash flow		$144,233	$260,235	$258,535	$349,622	$509,527	$552,347	$7,976,347
Present value		$128,779	$207,457	$184,020	$222,191	$289,119	$279,836	$4,041,066
Sum present value	$5,352,469							
Debt level*	$679,039							
Tentex equity	$4,673,430							
Liquidity discount rate	20.00%							
Discount due to liquidity	$934,686							
Equity less liquidity discount	$3,738,744							
Value of debt	$679,039							
Value of Tentex	$4,417,783							

*Market value of debt at the valuation date.

61

Tentex's after-tax equity and debt costs. As new capital additions are made, these assets are financed on an after-tax basis at 12 percent.

By discounting the expected free cash flows to the present at Tentex's cost of capital, the value of these cash flows is $5,352,469. The value of Tentex equity is this total less $679,039, or $4,673,430. One final adjustment needs to be made to this value. Remember that Tentex is a private firm, so its equity does not trade in a liquid market. Since the Tentex cost of capital was developed from factors that apply to firms whose equity trades in a liquid market, an adjustment must be made for the lack of liquidity, or marketability, of its equity.[9] In Chapter 6, we address this issue in much more detail, but for now we simply apply a discount of 20 percent for lack of marketability. This reduces the value of equity to $3,738,744. Adding back the initial value of debt yields a total value for Tentex of $4,417,783.

What Multiples Tell Us about the Value of Tentex

An important reason often given for using a multiples approach in conjunction with discounted free cash flow is to assess whether the latter yields a value consistent with market prices. In the analysis that follows, the equity multiple is used to calculate Tentex's equity value. The market value of debt is added to this value to obtain total firm value, which can also be calculated using the free-cash-flow-to-the-firm approach. The problem with using equity multiples is that it assumes that the multiples being used are directly applicable to the target firm. Let us explore whether this is indeed the case for Tentex.

Our search indicated that the comparable firms were all public companies. These firms operated in the same industry as Tentex, but each firm operated in slightly different industry segments. Nevertheless, Tentex and these comparable firms were generally impacted by the same economic and industry forces, and hence in this respect they offered useful valuation benchmarks. The data used in this analysis is shown in Table 4.6.

The comparable analysis we are about to undertake uses only the price-to-sales multiple as the valuation metric. While price-to-earnings (net income) multiples are often used as valuation metrics, these are characterized by a great deal of variability relative to the more stable revenue multiple. There are two reasons for this. First, sales are less subject to accounting distortions than earnings. Second, current earnings are far more variable than equity values, often leading to large year-to-year swings in the earnings multiple. Revenue, on the other hand, is generally far less variable than earnings, contributing to relatively less volatility in the revenue multiple. For these reasons, the revenue multiple is likely to be a better value metric to use as a standard of comparison than is the discounted free cash flow valuation.[10]

To place the comparable firms on a more equal footing relative to Tentex, we proceeded in two steps. In step 1, the value of g for each comparable

TABLE 4.6 Financial Information of Peer Firms

Company Name	Unlevered Beta	Reported Debt-to-Equity Ratio	Size Premium	Actual Levered Cost of Equity Capital	Cost of Equity: 90/10	Net Income Profit Margin	P/S Ratio	Implied g: Gordon Model	Adjusted Implied g	Estimated P/S
Cuno Inc.	0.4199	0.02	0.43%	8.40%	8.57%	9.30%	2.753	4.86%	3.00%	2.50
Esco Technologies, Inc.	0.4157	0.02	0.43%	8.37%	8.54%	6.74%	1.613	4.02%	2.00%	1.60
Flow International Corp.	0.4365	2.26	3.16%	15.60%	11.43%	-48.58%	0.272	-246.78%	NM†	NM
Nordson Corp.	0.3974	0.19	0.34%	8.45%	8.13%	5.27%	1.949	5.59%	4.60%	2.11
Pall Corp.	0.3846	0.18	0.34%	8.33%	8.20%	6.40%	1.857	4.72%	3.00%	1.85
Peerless Manufacturing Co.	0.4512	0.00	4.21%	12.38%	12.60%	-0.55%	0.458	13.74%	NM	NM
Taylor Devices, Inc.	0.4617	0.85	4.21%	14.21%	12.68%	2.53%	0.485	8.55%	8.00%	0.66
TB Woods Corp.	0.4512	0.65	4.21%	13.68%	12.60%	-0.37%	0.407	14.73%	NM	NM
Average*				11.18%	10.35%	6.05%	1.22	5.55%	4.12%	1.75
Tentex				15.00%	15.00%	10.79%		3.00%	3.00%	1.36‡

*Average based on positive values only. †Not meaningful. ‡Discounted cash flow multiple.

firm was determined and compared to the 3 percent used in the discounted free cash flow model. Each firm's g was solved for by assuming its price-sales ratio was established according to the Gordon-Shapiro model. This is termed the implied g. Then each firm's cost of equity capital was substituted into the Gordon-Shapiro model and each firm's implied g was solved for. As Table 4.6 indicates, the implied g for each firm was greater than 3 percent, with the average being almost twice as large, or 5.55 percent.

However, these two rates may not be fully consistent. The reason is that the differential could be a product of each firm having high near-term growth rates that are similar to Tentex, and yet the Gordon-Shapiro model forces these values to be averaged with the true long-term growth rate to produce an implied g that is greater than 3 percent.

To test this possibility, Equation 4.10 was solved for each comparable firm's adjusted implied g, designated as $\hat{g}_n$. The values of $g_1 \ldots g_6$ are equal to those used in the Tentex discounted free cash flow valuation.

$$
\begin{aligned}
V_0/R_0 = m_0 &\times [(1 + \hat{g}_1)/(1 + k)^1 + \ldots + (1 + \hat{g}_1) \times (1 + \hat{g}_2) \\
&\times \ldots \times (1 + \hat{g}_6)/(1 + k)^6 + (1 + \hat{g}_1) \times (1 + \hat{g}_2) \\
&\times \ldots \times (1 + \hat{g}_6) \times (1 + \hat{g}_n)/(k - \hat{g}_n)/(1 + k)^6]
\end{aligned}
\tag{4.10}
$$

$$V_0/R_0 = \text{revenue multiple}$$

The results of this analysis, although not shown separately, indicate that the average value of $\hat{g}_n$ is 4.12 percent. In step 2, a new cost of capital was calculated for each firm based on Tentex's target capital structure—90 percent equity and 10 percent debt.[11] Using the adjusted implied g, $\hat{g}_n$, and each firm's new equity cost of capital, each firm's estimated price-to-sales ratio was calculated assuming the Gordon-Shapiro model was operative. These values are shown in the column headed Estimated P/S in Table 4.6. The average of these values is 1.75, which is the average comparable multiple adjusted for Tentex's capital structure and each comparable firm's expected long-term growth in earnings. By comparison, the discounted cash flow equity multiple before an adjustment for marketability is 1.36.[12] This difference emerges because the values of the key parameters that determine the revenue multiple profit margin, near- and long-term earnings growth rates and the equity cost of capital, are significantly different for Tentex relative to the set of comparable firms. Nevertheless the comparable analysis did indicate that the long-term earnings growth may be greater than the 3 percent assumed for Tentex. To the extent that Tentex has potential for long-term earnings to grow at 4 percent instead of 3 percent, this should be factored into the valuation. We recalculated Tentex's discounted cash flow value using the 4 percent long-term growth rate. This raised the revenue multiple to 1.51, and the value of Tentex to $4,806,582, compared to the initial estimate of $4,673,430.

How does one reconcile these values? One way is to ask the question, what is the probability that Tentex's long-term growth will be 4 percent instead of 3 percent? Guidance for this determination should come from the valuation analyst's understanding of the nature of the business and the basis for the firm's competitive advantage. If we assume for the moment that this guidance suggested a 20 percent chance of achieving the 4 percent growth rate, and an 80 percent chance of a 3 percent growth rate, then Tentex's value would be equal to the weighted average of the two values, where the weights are the respective probabilities.

Tentex equity value = 0.8 × ($4,673,430) + 0.2($4,806,582) = $4,700,060

This analysis suggests that simply using the average or median of comparable multiples when the values of the key parameters of these firms do not match the values of these parameters for the target firm will result in firm values that are subject to a great deal of error. Since the long-term growth rate is an important determinant of firm value, comparable multiples can be used to gauge whether the long-term growth rate assumed for the target firm is consistent with investor expectations. This growth rate can then be used to recalculate the value of the firm using the discounted free cash flow approach. Finally, a weighted average of the two discounted free cash flow estimates can be calculated to determine the final value of the firm.

DISCOUNTED CASH FLOW OR THE METHOD OF MULTIPLES: WHICH IS THE BEST VALUATION APPROACH?

Discounted cash flow approaches are used routinely by Wall Street and buy-side analysts to value firms they view as potential investment candidates. Despite the acceptance of the discounted cash flow approach by the professional investment community, there is less support for its use by the valuation community that specializes in valuing private firms. A reason often given for this reluctance is that its use requires growth in revenue and earnings to be projected forward, and hence there is a great deal of uncertainty that surrounds these projections and the estimated value of the firm. By comparison, it appears on first glance that the method of multiples does not require the analyst to make any projections, but merely to carry out the required multiplication to calculate the value of the firm. However, as the preceding analysis indicates, this view is not correct. If the method of multiples is used without any adjustments to the parameters that determine its value, the valuation analyst is accepting projections that are embedded in the multiple being used. If these projections are inconsistent with the target firm's potential performance, the value placed on the target firm will be incorrect. Hence, both valuation metrics are subject to forecasting error. The question is which method is likely to be the most accurate? We now turn to the answer to this question.

Steven Kaplan and Robert Ruback performed an exhaustive study of this issue. The authors state:

> *Surprisingly, there is remarkably little empirical evidence on whether the discounted cash flow method or the comparable methods provide reliable estimates of market value, let alone which of the two methods provides better estimates. To provide such evidence, we recently completed a study of 51 highly leveraged transactions designed to test the reliability of the two different valuation methods. We chose to focus on HLTs [highly leveraged transactions]—management buyouts (MBOs) and leveraged recapitalizations—because participants in those transactions were required to release detailed cash flow projections. We used this information to compare prices paid in the 51 HLTs both to discounted values of their corresponding cash flow forecasts and to the values predicted by the more conventional, comparable-based approaches. We also repeated our analysis for a smaller sample of initial public offerings (IPOs), and obtained similar results.*[13]

The basic results of the Kaplan and Ruback study are shown in Table 4.7.

The researchers developed several estimates of value by combining projected cash flows that were available from various SEC filings with several estimates of the cost of capital developed using the capital asset pricing model, or CAPM (CAPM-based valuation methods). Beta, the centerpiece of the CAPM and a measure of systematic risk, was measured in three different ways. In Table 4.7, the median value of each beta type is in the Asset beta row. The Firm Beta column was measured using firm stock return information. The Industry Beta column was developed by aggregating firms into industries and then using industry return data to measure beta. The Market Beta column was estimated using return data on an aggregate market index.

The researchers defined comparable firms in three ways. The comparable firm method used a multiple calculated from the trading values of firms in the same industry. The comparable transaction method used a multiple from companies that were involved in similar transactions. The comparable industry transaction method used a multiple from companies that were both in the same industry and involved in a comparable transaction. Columns A through F show the errors associated with each valuation method. The firm beta–based

TABLE 4.7 Comparison of Free Cash Flow Valuation to the Method of Multiples

	CAPM-Based Valuation Methods			Comparable Valuation Methods		
	(A) Firm Beta	(B) Industry Beta	(C) Market Beta	(D) Comparable Company	(E) Comparable Transaction	(F) Comparable Industry Transaction ($N = 38$)
Panel A: Summary statistics for valuation errors						
1. Median	6.00%	6.20%	2.50%	−18.10%	5.90%	−0.10%
2. Mean	8.00%	7.10%	3.10%	−16.60%	0.30%	−0.70%
3. Standard deviation	28.10%	22.60%	22.60%	25.40%	22.30%	28.70%
4. Interquartile range	31.30%	23.00%	27.30%	41.90%	32.30%	23.70%
5. Asset beta (median)	0.81	0.84	0.91			
Panel B: Performance measures for valuation errors						
1. Pct. within 15%	47.10%	62.70%	58.80%	37.30%	47.10%	57.90%
2. Mean absolute error	21.10%	18.10%	16.70%	24.70%	18.10%	20.50%
Mean squarred error	8.40%	6.70%	5.10%	9.10%	4.90%	8.00%

discounted cash flow method had a median error of 6 percent. This means that the median estimated transaction value was 6 percent greater than the actual transaction price. The median errors for the industry and market betas were 6.2 percent and 2.5 percent, respectively. In comparison, the comparable company multiple had a median error of −18 percent, while the comparable transaction multiple had an error rate that was equivalent to the firm and industry beta discounted cash flow results. When the multiple reflects the industry and the transaction of the target firm, the error is close to zero.

While the multiple approaches seem to produce error rates similar to the discounted cash flow approach, further examination suggests that this is not the case. Column B in Table 4.7 indicates the percentage of transactions that were within 15 percent of the actual transaction price. The discounted cash flow method had a greater number of estimated transaction values within 15 percent of the actual transaction price than do the comparable approaches. The mean square error of the discounted cash flow approach is generally smaller than the mean square error for the comparable methods. The results taken together support the conclusion that the discounted cash flow is more accurate than a multiple approach, although the errors are likely to be lower if the methods are used together. Kaplan and Ruback conclude:

> *Although some of the "comparable" or multiple methods performed as well on an average basis, the DCF methods were more reliable in the sense that the DCF estimates were "clustered" more tightly around actual values (in statistical language, the DCF "errors" exhibited greater "central tendency"). Nevertheless, we also found that the most reliable estimates were those obtained by using the DCF and the comparable methods together.*[14]

SUMMARY

Several critical adjustments need to be made to the reported financial statements of private firms in order to properly calculate cash flow for valuation purposes. These include officer compensation and discretionary expense adjustments. If the firm has debt on the balance sheet, then the firm's reported tax burden must be increased by the tax shield on interest. NOPAT is calculated as taxable income less tax paid less the interest tax shield. Free cash flow equals NOPAT less change in working capital and net capital expenditures. Discounting expected free cash flow yields the value of the firm. Alternatively, the method of multiples can be used to value a private firm. Research suggests that the discounted free cash flow method is a more accurate valuation approach.

CHAPTER 5

Estimating the Cost of Capital

In addition to cash flow, firm value is also a function of the firm's cost of capital. This chapter covers how a private firm's cost of capital is calculated. The financial costs associated with financing assets is termed the *cost of capital* because it reflects what investors require in the form of expected returns before they are willing to commit funds. In return for funds committed, firms typically issue common equity, preferred equity, and debt. These components make up a firm's capital structure. Each of these components has a specific cost to the firm based on the state of the overall investment markets, the underlying riskiness of the firm, and the various features of each capital component. For example, a preferred stock that is convertible into common stock has a different capital cost than a preferred stock that does not have a conversion feature. Common stocks that carry voting rights have a lower cost of capital than common stocks that do not. This difference occurs because the common stock with voting rights is more valuable, and hence the return required on it is necessarily lower than the same common stock without voting rights.

A typical public firm has a capital structure that includes common equity and debt and, to a lesser extent, preferred stock. This contrasts to private firms, which generally have common stock and debt. S corporations, which represent the tax status of a significant number of private firms, cannot issue preferred stock. They can issue multiple classes of common stock, however.

The weighted average cost of capital (WACC) is calculated as the weighted average of the costs of the components of a firm's capital structure. The WACC for a firm that has debt (d), equity (e) and preferred equity (pe) is defined by Equation 5.1.

$$k_{\text{wacc}} = w_d \times k_d \times (1 - T) + w_e \times k_e + w_{pe}k_{pe} \qquad (5.1)$$

where w = the market value of each component of the firm's capital
structure divided by the total market value of the firm

k = the cost of capital for each component of the capital structure

T = the tax rate

The WACC is used in conjunction with the discounted free cash flow method, which was used in Chapter 4 to value Tentex. The sections that follow first focus on estimating the cost of equity capital. Although there are two competing theories of estimating the cost of capital, and equity capital in particular, the capital asset pricing model (CAPM) and arbitrage pricing theory (APT), this chapter focuses on an adjusted version of the CAPM known as the *buildup method*. The major reason is that this model is the one most often used by valuation analysts when estimating the cost of equity capital for private firms. Finally, we demonstrate how to estimate the cost of debt and preferred stock for private firms.

THE COST OF EQUITY CAPITAL

The basic model for estimating a firm's cost of capital is a modified version of the CAPM, as shown in Equation 5.2.

$$k_s = k_{rf} + \text{beta}_s[RP_m] + \text{beta}_{s-1}[RP_m]_{-1} + SP_s + FSRP_s \qquad (5.2)$$

where
k_s = cost of equity for firm s
k_{rf} = the 10-year risk-free rate
beta_s = systematic risk factor for firm s
beta_{s-1} = beta_s in the previous period
RP_m = additional return investors require to invest in a diversified portfolio of financial securities rather than the risk-free asset
$RP_{(m-1)}$ = RP in the previous period
SP_s = additional return investors require to invest in firm s rather than a large capitalization firm
$FSRP_s$ = additional return an owner of firm s requires due to the fact that the owner does not have the funds available to diversify away the firm's unique, or specific, risk

To estimate the cost of equity capital for firm s, values for the parameters in Equation 5.1 need to be developed. Ibbotson Associates is the source of several of these parameters.[1] The equity risk premium, RP_m, is calculated as the difference between the total return on a diversified portfolio of stock of large companies as represented by the NYSE stock return index, for example, and the income return from a Treasury bond that has

TABLE 5.1 Equity Risk Premiums for Various Time Periods

Time Period: Start Date	Period Dates	Equity Risk Premium
Depression	1932–2001	8.10%
War	1942–2001	8.30%
Recession	1982–2001	8.00%
Average		8.13%
Business cycle peak	1962–2001	4.80%
Business cycle peak	1972–2001	5.50%
Average		5.15%
Overall average		6.64%
Long-term risk premium	1926–2001	7.40%

20 years to mature. The income return is defined as the portion of the total return that comes from the bond's coupon payment. Table 5.1 shows the realized average equity risk premium through 2001 for different starting dates.

Table 5.1 indicates that the equity risk premium varies over different time spans. The risk premium required in Equation 5.1 equates to what an analyst would expect the risk premium to average over an extended future period. It appears from the preceding data that the risk premium values are higher when the starting point is in a recession or slow-growth year (e.g., 1932, 1982), and smaller when the starting point is in a high-growth year, relatively speaking (e.g., 1962, 1972). Ideally, the risk premium used in Equation 5.1 should reflect a normal starting and ending year rather than an extended period dominated by a unique set of events, like a war, for example.

CALCULATING BETA FOR A PRIVATE FIRM

Beta is a measure of systematic risk. Using regression techniques, one can estimate beta for any public firm by regressing its stock returns on the returns earned on a diversified portfolio of financial securities. For a private firm, this is not possible; the beta must be obtained from another source. The steps taken to calculate a private firm beta can be summarized as follows:

- Estimate the beta for the industry that the firm is in.
- Adjust the industry beta for time lag.

- Adjust the industry beta for the size of the target firm.
- Adjust the industry beta for the capital structure of the target firm.

Estimating the Industry Beta

Research indicates that firm betas are more variable than industry betas, and therefore systematic risk of a firm may be better captured using an industry proxy. Ibbotson Associates, a primary data source for industry betas, notes:

> *Because betas for individual companies can be unreliable, many analysts seek to calculate industry or peer group average betas to determine the systematic risk inherent in a given industry. In addition, industry or peer group averages are commonly used when the beta of a company or division cannot be determined. A beta is either difficult to determine or unattainable for companies that lack sufficient price history (i.e., non–publicly traded companies, divisions of companies, and companies with short price histories). Typically, this type of analysis involves the determination of companies competing in a given industry and the calculation of some sort of industry average beta.[2]*

Ibbotson Associates has developed betas by industry, as defined by SIC code. Firms included in a specific industry must have at least 75 percent of their revenues in the SIC code in which they are classified. Table 5.2 shows the Ibbotson data for SIC 3663, radio and television broadcasting equipment.[3]

The betas shown are for two size classes, an industry composite, which is akin to a weighted average of the firm betas that make up the industry, and the median industry beta. Ibbotson Associates also calculates levered and unlevered versions of the betas in Table 5.2. Since most firms in Ibbotson's data set are in multiple industries, Ibbotson has developed a process that captures this effect. Ibbotson refers to the product of this analysis as the *adjusted beta.*[4] The levered industry beta reflects the actual capital structure of the firms included in the industry, some of which have debt in their capital structure. By removing the influence of financial risk due to debt in the capital structure, one obtains the unlevered industry beta. This beta reflects only systematic business risk and not the financial risk that emerges because firms in the industry have debt in their capital structures. We return to the relationship between levered and unlevered betas in a subsequent section. For the moment we focus on the nonleverage adjustments that need to be made to the unlevered industry beta before it can used to estimate the cost of equity capital for a private firm.

TABLE 5.2 Statistics for SIC Code 3663

Radio and Television Broadcasting and Communications Equipment

This Industry Comprises 40 Companies

Sales ($ Millions)		Total Capital ($ Millions)	
Total	34,907.0	Total	34,170.0
Average	872.7	Average	854.3

Three Largest Companies		Three Largest Companies	
Motorola Inc.	30,004.0	Motorola Inc.	28,853.9
Scientific-Atlanta Inc.	1,671.1	Scientific-Atlanta Inc.	2,110.7
Allen Telecom Inc.	417.0	Tekelec	648.6

Three Smallest Companies		Three Smallest Companies	
Amplidyne Inc.	2.2	Electronic System Tech Inc.	1.9
Simtrol Inc.	1.9	Technical Communications CP	1.1
Electronic System Tech Inc.	1.3	Amplidyne Inc.	0.8

	Levered Betas		Unlevered Betas
	Raw Beta	Adjusted Beta	Adjusted Beta
Median	1.47	1.76	0.81
SIC composite	1.56	1.66	1.29
Large composite	1.53	1.63	1.26
Small composite	1.87	2.01	1.87

While Ibbotson has estimated betas for many industries, the industry coverage is by no means complete. Most private firms operate in detailed segments of industries covered by Ibbotson at a more aggregate level. The valuation analyst has three choices when the firm being valued is in an industry segment not covered by publicly available databases like Ibbotson Associates. First, one can choose to use a beta for a more aggregate industry that is related to the industry in which the target firm operates. The second choice is to assume the relevant beta is unity, since research suggests that betas drift toward the riskiness of the overall market. The third choice is to develop a model that estimates the beta for the disaggregate sector.

To see how one might implement this last option, we consider a version of the basic CAPM regression equation used to estimate beta, Equation 5.3.

$$k_l = \alpha_l + \text{beta}_l k_m + \varepsilon_l \tag{5.3}$$

where k_I = the return on a portfolio of firms operating in industry I
        k_m = the return on a broad market index (e.g., New York Stock Exchange Index)
     beta$_I$ = the measure of systematic risk for industry I
        α_I = a constant term
        ε_I = the regression error term

An analogous relationship to Equation 5.3 can be written where the percent change in operating earnings before tax for a segment of industry I, denoted as %PTI$_i$, is regressed against the percentage change in operating earnings for the overall economy, %PTI$_e$, as shown in Equation 5.4.

$$\%\mathrm{PTI}_i = \partial_i + \mathrm{beta}_i \,\%\mathrm{PTI}_e + \mu_i \tag{5.4}$$

We now assume that the beta for segment i is related to the beta of its more aggregate industry sector I plus a constant term related to the difference in systematic risk between the aggregate industry and its segment, as shown in Equation 5.5.

$$\mathrm{beta}_i = \mathrm{beta}_I + c_i \tag{5.5}$$

Substituting Equation 5.4 into Equation 5.5 and noting that beta$_I$ can be obtained from a source like Ibbotson gives rise to Equation 5.6.

$$\%\mathrm{PTI}_i - \mathrm{beta}_I \times \%\mathrm{PTI}_e = \partial_i + c_i \times \%\mathrm{PTI}_e + \mu_i \tag{5.6}$$

Axiom Valuation Solutions has constructed a time series for %PTI for 700 industries defined by SIC.[5] This data set was developed from multiple government sources. Using Axiom's data, Equation 5.6 was estimated. The final value of c_i was obtained using a two-stage procedure. This is done because many of the initial values of c_i from estimating Equation 5.6 were often implausibly high or low, and in some cases statistically insignificant. Such divergence is not surprising because the underlying Ibbotson and Axiom data come from different sources. To reduce the divergence and still capture the differential variability of beta within detailed industry segments, a second-stage regression was estimated for which the estimated industry c_i was the dependent variable, and c_i was then regressed against the aggregate industry beta and the standard deviation of the growth in industry-segment operating earnings. Equation 5.7 was the equation estimated, and Table 5.3 shows the results of this second-stage regression.

$$c_i = d_0 + d_1 \times \mathrm{beta}_I + d_2 \times \mathrm{std}\%\mathrm{PTI}_i + \theta_i \tag{5.7}$$

TABLE 5.3 Beta Decomposition Equation

Summary Output

	Regression Statistics
Multiple R	0.546048696
R square	0.298169178
Adjusted R square	0.296155317
Standard error	1.827726737
Observations	700

ANOVA

	df	SS	MS	F	Significance F
Regression	2	989.2034441	494.6017221	148.0584144	2.58229E-54
Residual	697	2328.387762	3.340585025		
Total	699	3317.591206			

	Coefficients	Standard Error	t-Stat	P-value	Lower 95%
Intercept	−0.300591958	0.156793904	−1.917115082	0.055631815	−0.60843667
Beta	−0.520569128	0.201171257	−2.587691385	0.009863351	−0.915543078
Standard deviation	3.584498155	0.210456798	17.03199038	1.197E-54	3.171293237

The regression results indicate that the coefficients are statistically significant. The explanatory power of the equation indicates that 30 percent of the variance in c_i is explained by the estimated cross-section relationship. Using the results of this two-step procedure, we can estimate $beta_i$ as Equation 5.8

$$beta_i = -0.30 + (1 - 0.52) \times beta_I + 3.58 \times std\%PTI_i \quad (5.8)$$

Now let us consider an example of how to use Equation 5.8. Assume we need to calculate beta for a firm in SIC 3317 (steel pipes and tubes), but have only the median unlevered beta for SIC 331 (steelworks, blast furnaces, and rolling and finishing mills), which is equal to 0.44. An approximation to the unlevered median industry beta for SIC 3317 is 0.52 as shown here.

$$beta_{3317} = -0.30 + (1 - 0.52) \times 0.44 + 3.58 \times (.017) = 0.52$$

Adjusting Beta for Size

The next step in estimating beta relates to adjusting the estimated median beta for size. Ibbotson and others have noticed that beta of small-company portfolios, though higher than for large-company portfolios were, nevertheless, not high enough to explain all of the excess return historically found in small stocks. Since private firms are generally smaller than the smallest public firms, this problem is likely to be magnified for them. One explanation for the small-firm beta bias is that small-firm stocks are often infrequently traded, so their share prices do not always move with the overall market. This would result in an estimated beta that would be biased downward. One way to remove or limit this bias is to estimate a lagged version of the capital asset pricing model.

$$k_s - k_{rf} = \partial_s + \text{beta}_s[\text{RP}_m] + \text{beta}_{s-1}[\text{RP}_m]_{-1} + \varepsilon_s \qquad (5.9)$$

Sumbeta is the term for $\text{beta}_s + \text{beta}_{s-1}$. Ibbotson Associates has estimated the sumbeta for 10 different-size classes based on market capitalization. Axiom Valuation Solutions has converted capitalization class sizes to sales class sizes and extended the class range to 15 beta and sumbeta-size classes. Table 5.4 shows the results of this analysis.

Now let us use the data in Table 5.4 to adjust the estimated beta for steel pipes and tubes. First note the relationship in Equation 5.10. The first term of the equation is the size factor. Note that it is symmetrical about the median value of 1.31 shown in the last row of Table 5.4. The second term is a factor that when multiplied by the size beta will yield the sumbeta. If we assume that Equation 5.10 holds approximately at the industry level, then we can use the values in the last column of Table 5.4 to adjust the median industry beta for target firm size and the beta lag effect.

$$\frac{\text{Size beta}}{\text{Median beta}} \times \frac{\text{sumbeta}}{\text{size beta}} = \frac{\text{sumbeta}}{\text{median beta}} \qquad (5.10)$$

An example will be helpful here. Assume one desires to estimate beta for a steel pipe and tube firm that has sales of slightly less than \$1 million. The median beta for this industry was estimated earlier to be 0.52. When this value is multiplied by 1.399, which is the factor for firms with less than \$1 million in revenue, the beta is increased to 0.73, which represents an increase in systematic risk of 40 percent.

Impact of Leverage on a Firm's Beta

Once the unlevered beta has been calculated, it can then be adjusted for the leverage of the firm being valued. To understand the impact of leverage on a firm's beta, we note the basic accounting identity shown in Equation 5.11.

$$\text{Assets} = \text{equity} + \text{debt} \qquad (5.11)$$

TABLE 5.4 Beta Size Adjustment

Size Beta	Percentile	Sum Size Beta	Percentile	Sales	Percentile	Ratio of Sumbeta to Size Beta	Percentile	Size Factor: Size Beta/Median Size Beta	Percentile	Beta Sum, Size × Size Factor	Percentile
1—largest	0.9100	1—largest	0.9100	1—largest	$22,225,812,786.89	1—largest	1	1—largest	0.69465649	1	0.6946565
2	1.0400	2	1.0600	2	$3,322,210,029.59	2	1.019231	2	0.79389313	2	0.8091603
3	1.0900	3	1.1300	3	$1,954,637,143.27	3	1.036697	3	0.83206107	3	0.8625954
4	1.1300	4	1.1900	4	$1,138,054,576.81	4	1.053097	4	0.86259542	4	0.9083969
5	1.1600	5	1.2400	5	$711,964,358.60	5	1.068966	5	0.88549618	5	0.9465649
6	1.1800	6	1.3000	6	$508,957,368.04	6	1.101695	6	0.90076336	6	0.9923664
7	1.2400	7	1.3800	7	$321,128,186.91	7	1.112903	7	0.94656489	7	1.0534351
8	1.2800	8	1.4800	8	$199,600,897.93	8	1.15625	8	0.97709924	8	1.129771
9	1.3400	9	1.5500	9	$185,000,000.00	9	1.156716	9	1.02290076	9	1.1832061
10a	1.4300	10a	1.7100	10a	$120,121,611.60	10a	1.195804	10a	1.09160305	10	1.3053435
10b	1.4100	10b	1.7100	10b	$41,913,488.23	10b	1.212766	10b	1.07633588	11	1.3053435
11	1.4239	11	1.7347	11	$31,900,000.00	11	1.218278	11	1.08693956	12	1.3241945
12	1.4378	12	1.7594	12	$21,900,000.00	12	1.223683	12	1.09754323	13	1.3430455
13	1.4517	13	1.7841	13	$11,900,000.00	13	1.228985	13	1.10814691	14	1.3618965
14	1.4656	14	1.8088	14	$1,000,000.00	14	1.234187	14	1.11875059	15	1.3807474
15	1.4795	15	1.8335	15	>$1,000.000	15	1.239291	15	1.12935427	16	1.3995984
Median	1.3100										

This accounting identity implies that the firm's asset beta is equal to the weighted average of the betas of the components of its capital structure, which in this case is made up of debt D and equity E. The equity and debt weights are the percent of the firm's assets financed with debt and equity, respectively, Equations 5.12 and 5.13.

$$\text{beta}_a = \left(\frac{E}{D+E}\right)\text{beta}_e + \left(\frac{D}{D+E}\right)\text{beta}_d \qquad (5.12)$$

$$\text{beta}_e = \text{beta}_a + \frac{D}{E}\,(\text{beta}_a - \text{beta}_d) \qquad (5.13)$$

Beta$_a$ is an indicator of the risk of the operating assets of the business. This beta is unrelated to how the assets of the firm are financed, and hence it is equivalent to the firm's unlevered beta, beta$_u$, shown in Equation 5.14. Noting that interest is a tax-deductible expense to the firm, and T being the tax rate, the relationship between the levered and unlevered beta can be written as shown in Equation 5.14.

$$\text{beta}_l = \text{beta}_u \times \left[1 + \left(\frac{D}{E}\right) \times (1-T)\right] - \text{beta}_d \times \left[\frac{D \times (1-T)}{E}\right] \quad (5.14)$$

If the debt beta is taken to be zero, Equation 5.14 can be written as Equation 5.15, which is known as the Hamada equation.[6]

$$\text{beta}_l = \text{beta}_u \times \left[1 + \left(\frac{D}{E}\right) \times (1-T)\right] \qquad (5.15)$$

Now let us calculate the levered beta assuming the size-adjusted unlevered beta is 0.73. If the market value of debt is $300,000, and the market value of equity is $700,000, then we can use Equation 5.16 to calculate the levered beta.

$$\text{beta}_l = 0.73 \times \left[1 + \left(\frac{\$300}{\$700}\right) \times (1-0.4)\right] = 0.73 \times (1+0.26) = 0.92 \quad (5.16)$$

A beta value of 0.92 represents the levered beta adjusted for size that should be used in Equation 5.1 to calculate the equity cost of capital. Note that this beta is in excess of 100 percent larger than the initial unlevered beta of 0.44. This difference effectively means that the cost of equity capital will be significantly higher than would be the case if the beta were not adjusted for industry segment, size, and the beta lag effect.

Size Premium

Ibbotson has shown that even after accounting for the unlevered beta size adjustment, small firms still earn excess returns, although these returns are

TABLE 5.5 Size Premiums for Size Premium Beta and Size Premium Sumbeta

Size Class	Sales	Size Premium (Beta)	Size Premium (Sumbeta)
1—largest	$22,225,812,786.89	0.16%	−0.34%
2	$3,322,210,029.59	0.95%	0.34%
3	$1,954,637,143.27	1.15%	0.43%
4	$1,138,054,576.81	1.56%	0.60%
5	$711,964,358.60	1.83%	0.79%
6	$508,957,368.04	2.03%	0.72%
7	$321,128,186.91	1.99%	0.52%
8	$199,600,897.93	2.66%	0.79%
9	$185,000,000.00	3.32%	1.38%
10—smallest	$120,121,611.60	6.76%	4.21%
Mid-cap, 3–5		1.37%	0.53%
Low-cap, 6–8		2.13%	0.65%
Micro-cap, 9–10		4.42%	2.28%

smaller when the sumbeta adjusted for size rather than simple size adjusted betas are used. Table 5.5 shows the differences in the size premiums when beta and sumbeta are used in the calculations.[7]

The size premium based on beta indicates that size is an important factor for firms with sales of less than $22 billion dollars. When the sumbeta is used, the size premium shows little variation through size class 8. The risk premium then rises significantly between class 8 and class 10. For example, when sales are about $200 million, the size premium is 0.79 percent, which is not much greater than for larger size classes. However, when sales decline by $80 million, the size premium increases to 4.21 percent. This suggests that the risk premium is likely to rise more than proportionately in relation to the decline in sales the lower the sales level, indicating that the risk premium for firms below $50 million in sales, for example, is likely to be quite large. The implication of this is that a valuation analyst using the smallest Ibbotson size premium when estimating the cost of capital for a firm that has $10 million in sales is more than likely to estimate a cost of capital that is too low, thereby producing an income-based valuation that is correspondingly too large.

How might a valuation analyst adjust the size premium for a small firm? In the absence of any additional information, one could increase the size premium by 3.42 percent (4.21% − 0.79%) for each $80 million decrement in sales. This would imply that a firm with $10 million in sales would have a size premium equal to 8.91 percent (4.21% + 3.42% + ($30M/$80M) × 3.42%). Because the relationship between the size-risk premium and sales size is likely to be nonlinear when sales are lower than $100 million dollars, the suggested correction may still understate the cost of capital for smaller private firms. At the moment, however, this likely the best that can be done to correct the cost-of-equity calculation for small firms.

The Firm-Specific Risk Premium

In standard finance theory, the equity cost of capital does not reflect firm-specific risk, because it is assumed that the risk unique to a firm can be diversified away. Thus, if the investor does not have to bear the risk, then the financial markets will not reward the investor for taking it. In estimating the cost of capital for a private firm, it is generally assumed that the owners cannot diversify away from the unique risk that the firm represents, and thus anybody desiring to purchase the firm would incorporate a premium to reflect this fact.

Firm-specific risk as it is generally understood refers to business risk that is associated with the unique characteristics of the firm. Table 5.6 shows some of the factors that would ordinarily be considered when assessing the magnitude of firm-specific risk. In this example, high risk, moderate risk, and low risk are given five points, three points, and one point, respectively. The weights given to each of the factors are arbitrary, although their relative values generally conform to the relative importance of the factors that most impact private firms. Many private firms have a great reliance on key personnel such that, if they were not available, the success of the business would be compromised. Hence, one would think that the weight given to this factor should be greater than 20 percent. It is not because this risk can be partially protected against through the purchase of key-person insurance. Hence, in part or in whole, the risk is diversifiable, thus the weighting reflects this possibility.

Now that the risk factors have been assessed and points determined, how does one go about relating the point total to the incremental return that a purchaser of the firm would require. As a matter of practice, the valuation analyst may have a rule that says if the point total is greater than 4 then the firm-specific risk premium is 5 percent. If the point total is between 3.1 and 3.9, then the risk premium would be set at 4 percent and so on. However, such a scheme is arbitrary.

To get an idea about the size of the firm-specific risk premium, one can review the returns earned on venture-capital funds. Venture capitalists raise money from diversified investors, pay a return consistent with the investment's systematic risk, and capture the resulting excess return. This additional return is what venture capitalists require to accept firm-specific risk of the firms in their funds.

Gompers and Lerner measure returns for a single private equity group from 1972 to 1997. Using a version of the CAPM, they find that additional

TABLE 5.6 Factors That Determine Firm-Specific Risk

	Firm-Specific Risk Matrix			
Risk Concept	Measurement	Assessment	Factor Weight	Weighted Assessment
Business stability	How long has the company been profitable? 1–3 years—High risk: 5 4–6 years—Moderate risk: 3 More than 6 years—Low risk: 1	High risk: 5	10.00%	0.50
Business transparency	Does the firm produce an audited financial statement at least once a year? Yes—Low risk: 5 No—High Risk: 1	Low risk: 1	10.00%	0.50
Customer concentration	Does the firm receive more than 30% of its revenue from less than 5 customers? Yes—High risk: 5 No—Low risk: 1	High risk: 5	25.00%	1.25
Supplier reliance	Can the firm change suppliers without sacrificing product/service quality or increasing costs? Yes—Low risk: 1 No—High risk: 5	High risk: 5	10.00%	0.50
Reliance on key people	Are there any personnel critical to the success of the business that cannot be replaced in a timely way at the current market wage? Yes—High risk: 5 No—Low risk: 1	High risk: 5	20.00%	1.00
Intensity of competition	What is the intensity of firm competition? Very intense—High risk: 5 Modestly intense—Moderate risk: 3 Not very intense—Low risk: 1	High risk: 5	25.00%	1.25
Sum			100.00%	5.00

return earned above the CAPM return was about 8 percent.[8] Cochrane studied all venture investments in the VentureOne database from 1987 through June 2000.[9] After adjusting the data for selection bias, he estimates an arithmetic average annualized return of 57 percent, with an arithmetic standard deviation of 119 percent. The beta of these funds was about unity, implying a return in excess of CAPM in the neighborhood of 40 percent. This return is likely to be too high, since it is not net of fees and other compensation that venture capitalists ordinarily receive. The return standard deviation also suggests a great deal of variability. Despite these shortcomings, it appears that firm-specific risk is significant and should be part of any cost of equity capital calculation.

THE COST OF DEBT

Like public firms, private firms have debt on the balance sheet. For newly issued debt at par, the cost is simply the coupon rate, or if it is bank debt, it is typically some function of the prime rate. Estimating the cost of debt becomes somewhat more difficult when the analyst needs to calculate the current cost of previously issued debt. This exercise can be carried out by undertaking a credit analysis of the firm in much the same way a bank credit analyst might do. One model that is very useful for this purpose is Altman's Z score model.[10] The steps in determining the cost of a private firm's debt using this model are:

- Estimate the firm's Z score using the Altman model.
- Convert the Z score to a debt rating.
- Determine the cost of debt for a given maturity as the rate on a Treasury security of equivalent maturity plus the expected yield spread of equivalent debt relative to the rate on the Treasury security.
- Add an additional risk premium to reflect firm size.

The Z score model for private firms is given by Equation 5.17.

$$Z = 0.717 \times X_1 + 0.847 \times X_2 + 3.107 \times X_3 + 0.42 \times X_4 + 0.998 \times X_5 \quad (5.17)$$

where $X_1 = \dfrac{\text{(current assets} - \text{current liabilities)}}{\text{total assets}}$

$X_2 = \dfrac{\text{retained earnings}}{\text{total assets}}$

$X_3 = \dfrac{\text{earnings before interest and taxes}}{\text{total assets}}$

$$X_4 = \frac{\text{book value of equity}}{\text{total liabilities}}$$

$$X_5 = \frac{\text{sales}}{\text{total assets}}$$

Table 5.7 shows the relationship between the firm's debt rating and its Z score by maturity of debt.

Using the Z score model, we can now calculate the cost of debt for Tentex, the private firm introduced in Chapter 4. Table 5.8 reproduces Tentex's balance sheet. Table 5.9 shows the calculation of Tentex's Z score. Tentex's Z score is 3.1, which translates to debt rated between C and B3/B– (refer to Table 5.7). The weighted average maturity of Tentex's debt is about 10 years. If the 10-year Treasury note rate is 4.68 percent, then based on Table 5.9, the rate on Tentex debt should be this rate plus 775 basis points (see Table 5.7), or 12.43 percent.

The 12.3 percent represents the rate that Tentex would be charged based solely on an analysis of its credit risk. The effective rate is likely to be larger, however, since loans to private businesses are typically secured by

TABLE 5.7 Relationship between, Z Score, Debt Rating, and Yield Spread

| | | Yield Spreads over like Maturity Treasuries: Basis Points | | | | | | |
| | | Maturity in Years | | | | | | |
Debt Rating	Z-Score	1	2	3	5	7	10	30
Aaa/AAA	8.15	5	10	15	22	27	30	55
Aa1/AA+	7.6	10	15	20	32	37	40	60
Aa2/AA	7.3	15	25	30	37	44	50	65
Aa3/AA–	7	20	30	35	45	54	60	70
A1/A+	6.85	30	40	45	60	65	70	85
A2/A	6.65	40	50	57	67	75	82	89
A3/A–	6.4	50	65	70	80	90	96	116
Baa1/BBB+	6.25	60	75	90	100	105	114	135
Baa2/BBB	5.85	75	90	105	115	120	129	155
Baa3/BBB–	5.65	85	100	115	125	133	139	175
Ba1/BB+	5.25	300	300	275	250	275	225	250
Ba2/BB	4.95	325	400	425	375	325	300	300
Ba3/BB–	4.75	350	450	475	400	350	325	400
B1/B+	4.5	500	525	600	425	425	375	450
B2/B	4.15	525	550	600	500	450	450	725
B3/B–	3.75	725	800	775	750	725	775	850
Caa/CCC	2.5	1500	1600	1550	1400	1300	1375	1500

Source: Altman and BondsOnline Corporate Yield-Spread Matrix.

TABLE 5.8   Tentex's Balance Sheet

Row	Concepts Assets	2003		2002	Change: 2003/2002
1	Cash	$220,000		$187,000	
2	Cash required for operations	$71,251		$64,126	
3	Excess cash	$148,749		$122,874	
4	Accounts receivable	$356,256		$302,817	
5	Inventories	$890,639		$846,107	
6	Other current assets	$0		$0	
7	Total current assets	$1,686,895		$1,522,924	
8	Gross plant and equipment	$5,343,834		$5,076,642	
9	Accumulated depreciation	$3,730,729		$3,480,729	
10	Net fixed capital	$1,613,105		$1,595,914	
11	Total assets	$3,300,000		$3,118,838	
12	Liabilities and Equity				
13	Short-term debt and current portion of long-term debt	$200,000		$190,000	
14	Accounts payable	$178,128		$160,315	
15	Accrued liabilities	$50,000		$42,500	
16	Total current liabilities	$428,128		$392,815	
17	Long-term debt	$490,000		$454,151	
18	Other long-term liabilities	$0		$90,000	
19	Deferred income taxes	$0			
20	Total shareholder equity	$2,381,872		$2,181,872	
21	Total liabilities and equity	$3,300,000		$3,118,838	
22	Working capital	$890,018	$0	$820,235	$69,783
23	Net fixed capital	$1,613,105	$0	$1,595,914	$17,192
24	Net capital requirements				$86,974
25	NOPAT	$362,201			
26	Interest expense	$55,800			
27	Income available to shareholders and creditors	$418,001			
28	Free cash flow to the firm (row 27–row 24)	$331,026			

TABLE 5.9   Tentex Z Score

Z Score Model Variables	(Current Assets Current Liabilities)/ Assets	Accumulated Retained Earnings/ Assets*	EBIT/ Assets	Book Value Equity/Total Liabilities	Sales/ Assets
Value of Variables	0.38	0.14	0.21	2.59	1.08
Coefficient from Z Score Model	0.717	0.847	3.107	0.42	0.998
Weighted Value (coefficient* variable value)	0.27	0.12	0.65	1.09	1.08
Z Score	3.21				

*Accumulated retained earnings is 20 percent of shareholder equity.

business assets and/or the personal guarantee of the owners. In addition, some lenders require an additional yield depending on firm size. The logic behind this premium is that smaller firms are inherently more risky than equivalent larger firms, even when their credit risk profiles are equal. This phenomena is consistent with the way the equity markets assess systematic risk, with smaller firms having a greater cost of equity capital than their larger-firm counterparts, all else equal (other than firm size).

Although we are not aware of evidence of this size bias, the SBA 7(a) program offers some insight on what the size premium might be. The 7(a) program requires partner banks to set small business loan rates based on the prime rate plus anywhere between 2.75 and 4.75 percent. While the SBA does not refer to these differentials as size premiums, the fact that the SBA guarantees a portion of the loan, up to 85 percent, and requires that borrowers personally guarantee the loan, in addition to the firm providing collateral, suggests that these differentials in part or in total are related to firm size.[11] In Tentex's case, if it refinanced its $690,000 in loans outstanding based on the preceding facts, the likelihood is that the market rate would be in the neighborhood of 15.18 percent (12.43% + 2.75%) to 17.18 percent (12.43% + 4.75%).

Based on an interest rate of 15.18 percent (7.6% compounded semiannually) and interest payments over a 10-year period of $55,000 per year, principal repayment of $690,000, the market value of Tentex's debt can be calculated using Equation 5.18.

$$D_{\text{TENTEX}} = \sum_{t=1}^{20} \frac{(\$27,500)_t}{(1 + 0.076)^t} + \frac{\$717,500}{(1 + 0.076)^{10}} = \$438,179 \qquad (5.18)$$

If the interest rate were 17.18 percent, the market value of Tentex's debt would be $391,303. When using the discounted free cash flow model, the market value of debt would be calculated in this way.[12]

TABLE 5.10 Preferred Stock Returns versus Common Stock Returns

	Preferred Stock	Average Monthly Return: 1998—01.2003	Common Stock	Average Monthly Return: 1998—01.2003
1	FORD MOTR PRT (NYSE:F_pt)	0.47%	Ford	-1.52%
2	BARCLAYS BK PR	0.58%	BCS (BARCLAYS PLC)	0.78%
3	GAB_P (GABELLI EQ PR)	0.64%	GBL (GABELLI ASSET A)	2.20%
4	DYNEX CAPTL PRB (NasdaqNM:DXCPO)	2.05%	DYNEX CAPITAL (NYSE:DX)	1.11%
5	J.P. MORGAN PR A (NYSE:JPM_pa)	0.38%	JPM (JP MORGAN CHASE)	0.68%
6	CAMECO CORP PR	0.79%	CCJ (CAMECO CORP)	1.43%
7	CCM_P (CARLTON COMM PR)	0.66%	CCTVY (CARLTON COMM)	-0.47%
8	INTEGRA CAP PR	0.36%	INTEGRA BANK CP (NasdaqNM:IBNK)	-0.52%
9	MARINER CAP PR (NasdaqNM:FMARP)	0.58%	FST MARINER (NasdaqNM:FMAR)	2.61%
10	OI_PA (OWENS ILL PR A)	1.17%	OI (OWENS-ILLINOIS)	2.58%
11	NCX_P (NOVA CHEM CP PR)	0.59%	NOVA CHEMICALS (NYSE:NCX)	1.58%
12	ANZ_P (AUSTRALIA NZ PR)	0.52%	ANZ BANKING GRP (NYSE:ANZ)	1.57%
13	ROYCE VAL PR (NYSE:RVT_p)	0.61%	RVT (ROYCE VALUE TR)	0.90%
14	LKFNP (LAKELAND CAP PR)	0.65%	LAKELAND FINL (NasdaqNM:LKFN)	1.22%
15	IFC_PP (IFC CAP I PR P)	0.68%	IFC (IRWIN FINL CORP)	0.76%
16	SQA_P (SEQUA CORP PR)	0.23%	SEQUA CORP A (NYSE:SQAa)	-0.17%
17	ABANP (ABI CAP TR PR)	0.73%	APPLIED BIOSYS (NYSE:ABI)	1.47%
18	MER_PC (MERRILL PR C)	0.64%	MER (MERRILL LYNCH)	0.84%
19	N_PE (INCO PR E)	1.53%	N (INCO LTD)	2.56%

20	PCR_P (PERINI CORP PR)	0.12%	PERINI CORP (AMEX:PCR)	0.77%
21	WIS_P (WISCONSIN PWR PR)	0.71%	WISCONSIN ENER (NYSE:WEC)	0.11%
22	WHX_P (WHX CORP PR A)	−1.60%	WHX (WHX CORP)	−1.30%
23	VVI_P (VIAD CORP PR)	0.36%	VVI (VIAD CORP)	−0.16%
24	SOR_P (SOURCE CAPITAL)	0.78%	SOR (SOURCE CAPITAL)	0.64%
25	PFP_P (PREM FARNELL PR)	1.21%	PFP (PREM FARNELL)	1.80%
26	ALE_P (ALLETE PR)	0.74%	ALE (ALLETE INC)	0.58%
27	HOUSEHOLD PR P (NYSE:HI_pp)	0.67%	HI (HOUSEHOLD INTL)	−0.07%
28	HARRIS PR CAP (NYSE:HBC_p)	0.57%	HRS (HARRIS CORP)	0.61%
29	SO_PB (STHRN CO IV PR B)	0.56%	SO (SOUTHERN CO)	1.74%
30	CALLON PETR PR A (NYSE:CPE_pa)	0.85%	CPE (CALLON PETROLEUM)	−0.37%
31	GOODRICH CO A (NYSE:GR_pa)	0.66%	GR (GOODRICH CORP)	−0.32%
32	AGU_P (AGRIUM PR)	0.80%	AGU (AGRIUM INC)	1.03%
33	FMS_P (FRESENIUS MED PR)	−0.08%	FMS (FRESENIUS MEDCL)	−0.16%
34	KAN-CITY SO PR (NYSE:KSU_p)	1.04%	KSU (KANSAS CITY SO)	0.75%
35	LQL_P (LA QUINTA PPY PR)	1.61%	LQI (LA QUINTA CORP)	0.35%
36	NHI_P (NATL HEAL PR)	1.30%	NHI (NATL HEALTH INV)	0.88%
37	OLP_P (ONE LIBERTY PROP)	0.97%	OLP (ONE LIBERTY)	1.31%
38	TRP_P (TRANSCANADA PR)	0.60%	TRP (TRANSCANADA PIPE)	0.94%
39	TTN_P (TITAN CORP PR)	2.17%	TTN (TITAN CORP)	4.74%
40	GDPAP (GOODRICH PRA)	2.63%	GDP (GOODRICH PETE)	4.35%
	Average return across firms	0.7634%		0.9460%

THE COST OF PREFERRED STOCK

Preferred stock is a hybrid security that has features of both debt and equity. Preferred stock cannot be issued by S corporations. In contrast, C corporations can issue preferred stock. In case of bankruptcy, preferred stockholders are paid before common stockholders, and therefore a firm's preferred stock is less risky than its common. The dividend on preferred stock represents an obligation of the corporation, and in this sense it is like interest payments on debt. While interest payments are a legal obligation of the firm, preferred dividends are akin to a moral obligation. If the firm does not pay the preferred dividend, the owner of the preferred stock cannot legally force the firm to pay it, and in this respect the preferred stock is like common equity. Typically, however, preferred dividends are cumulative. Preferred stock that is convertible to common stock is termed *convertible preferred*. The value of this preferred is equal to the value of a nonconvertible of equal risk plus the value of the conversion feature, which is a call option on the equity of the firm. Here, we value only a straight preferred. The cost of preferred equity is given by Equation 5.19.

$$V_{ps} = \frac{div_{ps}}{k_{ps}} \qquad (5.19)$$

Since V_{ps} is not known for a private firm, k_{ps} cannot be calculated from Equation 5.19. Therefore, we need to calculate k_{ps} using another approach. Since preferred stock is less risky than common, k_{ps} should be lower then k_e. This suggests that if we know the ratio of the average preferred stock return to the average common stock return then we can calculate k_e using the buildup method and then multiply the result by the return ratio to estimate k_{ps}. Table 5.10 estimates the return ratio using a sample of 40 firms.

The data indicates that the preferred stock return on average is about 80 percent of the common stock return. Thus we can approximate the preferred stock return by multiplying the common stock return, estimated using the adjusted CAPM, by 80 percent. If the cost of equity is 25 percent, then the cost of a straight preferred can be approximated by 0.8×25 percent, or 20 percent.

Calculating the Weighted Average Cost of Capital

Table 5.11 shows an example of estimating the weighted average cost of capital for a firm that has $10 million in revenue.

The WACC is 25 percent. This rate is dominated by the cost of equity, because the capital structure assumed is 90 percent equity and 10 percent debt. As the debt percentage rises, the WACC will decline because the after-tax cost of debt is lower than the cost of equity. As noted in Chapter 2, as

TABLE 5.11 Weighted Average Cost of Capital for a $10 Million Revenue Firm

Row	Cost of Capital Components	Values	Source
1	Risk-free rate	4.68%	Text
2	Unlevered beta	0.52	Text
3	Beta adjustment factor for size and sum	1.37	Linear interpolation of values in Table 5.4
4	Unlevered beta adjusted for size and sum	0.71	Calculated, text
5	Debt/equity ratio	11.11%	90% equity, 10% debt: assumed
6	Tax rate	0.4	Statutory
7	Levered beta adjusted for size and sum	0.76	Calculated, equation 5.15
8	Risk premium	7.42%	Table 5.1
9	Size premium	8.91%	Text and Table 5.5
10	Firm-specific risk premium	8.00%	Text: Gompers and Learner
11	Cost of equity	27.23%	Calculated, Equation 5.2
12	Debt cost	8.21%	Tentex example
13	Cost of preferred stock	21.78%	Text
14	Equity percentage	90.00%	Assumed
15	Debt percentage	10.00%	Assumed
16	Preferred stock percentage	0.00%	Assumed
17	WACC	25.00%	Calculated, Equation 5.1

more debt is used in the capital structure, the WACC will reach a minimum and then begin to rise. This occurs because at some point the additional risk created by the additional debt issued, measured as the increase in the present value of bankruptcy costs, is greater than the tax benefits from the incremental debt issuance.

SUMMARY

This chapter addressed the issues in estimating the weighted average cost of capital and its components—the cost of equity, debt, and preferred stock. Using the buildup method, we estimated the cost of equity and proposed a method to make several adjustments to Ibbotson size premium to make it more useful in estimating the cost of equity for private firms. Altman's Z score model was used to estimate the base cost of debt for a private firm. To this value an increment was added based on firm size to obtain the final cost of debt. Finally, the cost of preferred stock was estimated by demonstrating that, on average, the preferred stock return is about 80 percent of the return on common equity.

CHAPTER 6

The Value of Liquidity

Estimating the Size of the Liquidity Discount

Firm A is a closely held firm whose securities are not listed on a highly liquid exchange such as the New York Stock Exchange (NYSE). Firm B is equivalent in every way to Firm A except that its shares trade on the NYSE. Assuming that the financial prospects of both firms are known to both private and public market participants, Firm A shares will trade at a discount to those of Firm B because shares of the former are far less liquid than those of the latter. This discount is known as the *liquidity* or *marketability discount.*[1]

The valuation of closely held firms is often carried out in two steps. First, the securities are valued as though they trade on a highly liquid exchange. Second, this value is reduced by the size of the estimated liquidity discount. The size of this discount has been debated, with almost no consensus on how to estimate it or what a plausible range might be. Indeed, the measured size of this discount has ranged from a value exceeding 40 percent to as small as 7.2 percent. This chapter reviews some of the more important research by financial economists and uses the results of this review to establish a plausible range for the size of the liquidity discount. Our analysis suggests five fundamental conclusions:

1. When valuing minority shares of a privately held C corporation, the liquidity discount should be in the neighborhood of 17 percent.
2. Minority shares of S corporations are less liquid than shares of an equivalent C corporation.
3. Hence, discounts applied to minority S shares should be greater than discounts applied to minority C shares.
4. When valuing control shares of a freestanding C corporation, discounts should be in the neighborhood of 20 percent and incrementally higher for S shares.
5. Discounts in excess of 30 percent for either minority or control shares are simply not supported by peer-reviewed research.

DOES LIQUIDITY AFFECT ASSET PRICES? SETTING THE STAGE

Studying the pricing effects of liquidity is a major issue in both theoretical and empirical finance. While lack of liquidity affects the value of private securities, it also influences the prices of securities that trade in organized markets. Financial research has even suggested that portfolios of less liquid stocks provide investors with significantly higher returns, on average, than highly liquid stock portfolios, even after adjusting for risk.[2] This research suggests that the liquidity factor may be as important as risk in determining stock returns. Yakov Amihud and Haim Mendelson also note that higher returns on less liquid securities translate to a price discount relative to more liquid securities:

> *Why does liquidity affect stock returns? The most straightforward answer is that investors price securities according to their returns net of trading costs; and they thus require higher returns for holding less liquid stocks to compensate them for the higher costs of trading. Put differently, given two assets with the same cash flows but with different liquidity, investors will pay less for the asset with lower liquidity.*[3]

The size of the price concession due to lack of liquidity and the factors that determine it are of special interest to those who value private securities. Unlike the public firm discount literature, the interest in the size of the discount applicable to private securities is primarily, although not exclusively, related to on-the-ground practical issues. These include what the IRS will allow when valuing private shares for estate planning purposes, charitable gifting, and estimating capital gains taxes due when private firms are transacted. Since there is a great deal of controversy surrounding some of the more common liquidity benchmarks, valuation analysts are always concerned that the value applied will, at worst, be contested by the IRS or, at the very least, seriously questioned. To begin our analysis, we appeal to a liquidity literature that has not generally been brought to bear on the debate of the size of liquidity discount as it relates to privately held securities.

MEASURING ILLIQUIDITY IN THE PUBLIC SECURITY MARKETS

Availability of liquidity is a key determinant of asset prices in public security markets. Organized exchanges, like the New York Stock Exchange, create liquid trading environments because they offer investors a number of benefits:

- Establishing a set of rules for listing a security on an exchange.
- Ensuring that the number of shares available to be exchanged is a significant percentage of the total available.
- Ensuring that the firms listed meet minimum standards of financial performance and that their information disclosure is consistent with SEC requirements.
- Ensuring that the costs of transacting are low relative to the price of an average share.
- Ensuring that the costs associated with listing are low relative to the liquidity benefits that accrue to the shareholders of the listing firm.

In a perfect exchange world, market participants would have full information about the securities being exchanged, prices would reflect this information, and bid-asked spreads would be a tiny percentage of the bid price. Thus, the spread would reflect only the production costs of executing a transaction. In this stylized world, there are no information asymmetries. Prices of securities are therefore efficiently priced; that is, security prices reflect all known information about risks and opportunities. In the real world, things are not this tidy.

The public security markets are made up of *auction markets,* such as the New York Stock Exchange (NYSE), where prices are directly determined by buyers and sellers, and *dealer markets,* such as the over-the-counter (OTC) market, where a network of dealers stand ready to buy and sell securities at posted prices. Transactions not handled on large liquid auction markets like the NYSE are handled in the OTC market. This market primarily handles unlisted securities, or securities not listed on a stock exchange, although some listed securities do trade in the OTC market. Securities of more than 35,000 firms are traded in this market, most of which are thinly traded, highly illiquid stocks that do not have a significant following. Prices of these stocks may be reported once per day or even less frequently on what is termed *pink sheets,* hence the name *pink sheet stocks.* Prior to the establishment of the Nasdaq Stock Market, OTC firms could obtain the benefits of maximum liquidity only if they could list their shares on the NYSE. At one time, the major benefit of moving from the OTC to the NYSE was that the greater liquidity of the NYSE would result in a higher share price, all else equal. The ratio of the resulting price increase to the NYSE price is equal to the price of liquidity, or the *liquidity discount.* For example, if an OTC-listed firm were to list on the NYSE, and the share price increased by $1 per share on the announcement date, say from $20 to $21, then the price of liquidity would be 4.8 percent ($1 ÷ $21).

Although increased liquidity may be the primary reason a share price increases when a firm moves from the OTC to the NYSE, it is also possible that the increase is a result of *information signaling*. In such case, when a firm is accepted to list on the NYSE, it is akin to having a seal of approval. As a result, investors conclude that expected future financial results are now more certain. This means that the listing signal has high informational value, which leads to greater certainty about future firm performance in the postlisting environment, a lower cost of equity capital, and therefore a higher share price. Thus, the price increase and the implied discount that results when firms move from quasi-private-firm status like the OTC to listing on a major exchange may be, in part or completely, the product of information signaling.

Several important strands of research shed light on these issues, and an examination of each will help us place boundaries on the price of liquidity. However, before presenting these results, we need to review a basic research design used by financial economists so that their reported results can be interpreted properly.

EVENT STUDY METHODOLOGY

To study the impact of a particular event on share prices, researchers have developed an event study methodology. This method isolates the impact of the event, in this case the listing announcement, on the listing stock's return. To implement the procedure properly, all confounding events around the *event window,* a period prior and subsequent to the event date, need to be controlled for. Confounding events include movements in the overall market and/or firm-specific events like acquisitions or divestitures. If an acquisition or other major firm-specific event takes place within the event window, the firm is usually removed from the sample or, if kept, the researcher uses some other approach to control for the influence of the confounding event on the study's results. The firms that remain are those whose share prices have changed because the overall market moved or because of the event being studied, which in this case is the listing announcement.

To remove the influence of movements in the overall market, re-searchers calculate an abnormal return, which is defined in Equation 6.1.

$$AR_{jt} = R_{jt} - (\hat{a}_j + \hat{B}_j \times R_{mt}) \tag{6.1}$$

where AR_{jt} = abnormal return, stock j at time t
R_{jt} = rate of return, stock j at time t
$\hat{B}_j$ = estimated beta, firm j
R_{mt} = rate of return, market index
$\hat{a}_j$ = constant term from regression model used to estimate beta

Event studies require the measurement of returns on a daily or weekly basis around the event date. If P_b and P_a are prices before and after the event, respectively, then P_a is equal to $P_b \times (1 + AR_a)$. The ratio of P_b/P_a is $1/1 + AR_a$ so the implied discount is $1 - (1/1 + AR_a)$, or $AR_a/(1 + AR_a)$. Therefore, if the abnormal return is measured as 20 percent, then the liquidity discount is $(0.20/1.20) \times 100 = 16.7$ percent.

Using event study methodology, Gary C. Sanger and John J. McConnell studied the impact on abnormal returns of OTC stocks that listed on the NYSE over the period 1966–1977.[4] This period spans the introduction of the National Association of Securities Dealers Automated Quotations (Nasdaq) system in the OTC market. For our purposes, of particular interest is the magnitude of the abnormal return responses for firms moving to the NYSE from the OTC prior to the introduction of Nasdaq.[5] These results are reported in Table 6.1, which shows abnormal returns over the event window, 52 weeks prior to the listing event (week 0) and 52 weeks subsequent to it. The cumulative abnormal return registered an increase long before the event and reached its maximum about 8 weeks after the event. In efficient security markets, we would expect the bulk of the increase to occur around the announcement date. The abnormal return pattern indicates a very slow information diffusion process during the 1966–1970 period. This is no surprise, however. During this time period, markets were highly inefficient because of lack of technology and the high cost of obtaining and processing information. Hence, a liquidity adjustment took far longer to impact share prices at that time than would a similar event today. But it is precisely this type of lab experiment that one needs to evaluate, because going from pink sheet status during the 1966–1970 period is closely akin to a private firm listing on a public market today.

The cumulative abnormal return reached a maximum of 0.2663 (26.63 percent) eight weeks after the listing announcement, then tapered off to 0.2568 (not shown) one year after the event. If we conclude that, on average, share prices of firms in the sample rose by 25 percent as a result of moving from the OTC to the NYSE, then this implies a discount of 20 percent.

The question remains, how much of this share price increase is due to improved liquidity and how much is due to information signaling? To better understand the influence of each determinant, we turn to a paper by Richard Edelman and Kent Baker.[6] Their study examined market behavior of common stocks transferring from the Nasdaq Stock Market to the NYSE from 1982 to 1989. Using event study methodology, the authors show that stocks that are characterized by low liquidity (wide bid-asked spreads) and high informational signaling value (expected poor earnings prospects during the prelisting period) have a cumulative abnormal return of 7 percent, or a discount of 6.5 percent. Since firms on the Nasdaq that make the transition

TABLE 6.1 Summary of Abnormal Returns Analysis of 153 OTC Stocks That Listed on the NYSE over the Period 1966–1970 for the 105 Event Weeks Surrounding the Week of Announcement

Event Week (a)*	Average Abnormal Return	Z Statistic	Cumulative Average Abnormal Return (d), Begins in week –52	Percent Nonnegative
–9	0.0108	3.01[†]	0.1639	0.58[†]
–8	0.0087	2.52[‡]	0.1725	0.56[†]
–7	0.0079	2.15[‡]	` 0.1804	0.52
–6	0.0079	2.06[‡]	0.1883	0.51
–5	–0.0018	–0.62	0.1865	0.42
–4	0.006	1.7	0.1925	0.54*
–3	0.0003	0.3	0.1928	0.46
–2	0.0056	1.5	0.1984	0.53[‡]
–1	0.0104	2.73[†]	0.2088	0.51
0	0.0088	2.44[‡]	0.2176	0.52
1	0.0088	2.32[‡]	0.2263	0.52
2	0.0012	0.52	0.2275	0.45
3	0.0031	0.78	0.2306	0.49
4	0.0098	2.76[†]	0.2404	0.52
5	0.0116	2.55[‡]	0.252	0.52
6	–0.0003	–0.31	0.2517	0.48
7	0.0064	2.19[‡]	0.2581	0.48
8	0.0082	1.62	0.2663	0.51

*(a) Week relative to the week of listing on the NYSE.
[†]Significant at the 0.01 level.
[‡]Significant at the 0.05 level.

to the NYSE are likely to be followed by multiple analysts and therefore have low informational signaling value during the prelisting period, it is more than likely that the price increase is a direct result of greater liquidity. This is further supported by the fact that charters of many mutual and pension funds preclude them from investing in non-NYSE-listed stocks. By moving to the NYSE, firms significantly increase the demand for their stock by the institutional investor community. Hence, one can reasonably conclude that the average 7 percent price rise is predominately due to greater liquidity during the postlisting period. If we assume that moving from pink sheet status to the Nasdaq has the same liquidity benefit that moving from the Nasdaq to the NYSE does, then moving from the OTC to the NYSE amounts to a minimum 14 percent price appreciation, with the remaining 11 percent (25% – 11%) due to information signaling. This 14 percent translates into a discount of 12.3 percent. This means that the pure liquidity affect on a minority share of stock listed on the OTC results in a price discount of 12.3 percent relative to its price if it were trading on the NYSE. Since a minority share of stock of a closely held firm is more illiquid than a share of an equivalent firm listed on the OTC, the discount applied to the former should be in excess of 12 percent. But what should the size of the private firm discount increment be? Put differently, what is the liquidity premium a share would command by moving from closely held status to pink sheet status? One might argue that the discount should be no smaller than the discount associated with moving from the OTC to the Nasdaq. This means that a share of equity of a firm trading on the NYSE would sell at a minimum 21 percent premium to the equity share of an equivalent closely held firm. Alternatively, this 21 percent premium translates into a 17 percent liquidity discount (0.21/1.21). But to what extent do these results compare with other reported results on the size of the liquidity discount?

STUDIES OF THE LIQUIDITY DISCOUNT

The most often quoted studies of the liquidity discount include the pre-IPO studies of John D. Emory and the restricted studies of William L. Silber and Michael Hertzel and Richard Smith.[7] Emory consistently reports median discounts that exceed 40 percent, while simple simulations of Silber's regression model indicate discounts of 35 percent or more. Herzel and Smith report a coefficient of 13.5 in their regression that can be interpreted as a restricted stock discount due to illiquidity of 13.5 percent. The first question that arises is, why is there so much disparity in the reported results? Let us briefly address this issue.

IPO Studies

Emory's work compares equity values when firms were private to their subsequent IPO prices. He asserts that the percent difference between a firm's private equity value and its IPO price is the discount for lack of marketability. Emory finds that the greater the time period between the IPO and the valuation date when the firm was private, the greater the marketability discount.

There are several serious problems with Emory's research design. First, the private transactions are with insiders and are generally not done at arm's length. These prices are often reduced to reflect compensation to insiders. Moreover, the transactions do not represent a cash transaction, so the price base to which the IPO price is compared is likely to be too low and the discount too large. Second, Emory does not adjust the equity reference price (pre-IPO price) to which he compares the IPO price for changes in the overall stock market or for the time value of money between the reference and IPO dates. Hence, if the overall market were generally rising over the measurement interval, the discount would be biased upward. Even if the market did not move between the reference and IPO dates, the IPO price would be higher due to the time value of money. That is, if a private transaction established a $10 share price today, all else equal, this same share would be worth more in the future simply because of the time value of money. At a minimum, the base prices used by Emory should be adjusted upward by the time value factor. This would raise the private transaction price and reduce the size of the reported discount. In short, the results of the various Emory studies are not accurate estimates of discounts for lack of liquidity.

What Do Private Placement Studies Tell Us?

Firms that have issued equity in the public security markets, for a variety of reasons, also sell equity in the private placement market. By comparing the private placement issue price to the equity price in the public market, one can measure the private placement discount. Sales to the private market include (1) securities that are registered and thus have few, if any, transaction restrictions and (2) restricted securities issued under SEC Rule 144. Rule 144 permits an investor to sell limited quantities of stock in any three-month period. Restrictions on reselling of restricted stock were originally set to expire two years after the original acquisition. In February 1997, the restricted period was reduced to one year. Hence restricted private equity, all else equal, is less liquid than private placement equity that does not have these restrictions.

In the liquidity discount literature, it has been assumed that the restricted stock discount emerges due to lack of liquidity. Silber notes that "companies issuing restricted stock alongside registered securities trading in the open market usually offer a price discount in the restricted securities to compensate for their relative illiquidity." However, there are other reasons why a restricted stock discount might exist. From the supply side, the purchasers of privately placed securities, including restricted stock, are very often large institutions like life insurance companies and pension funds. These buyers have a long-term investment horizon and therefore place a low value on liquidity. Given their investment preferences, it is not sensible to think they would require a deep discount to purchase stock that would be illiquid for only two years. So, if illiquidity is not the primary or even the secondary reason for the discount, then why does it exist at all?

Research by S. C. Myers and N. S. Majluf supports the view that the private placement market offers an opportunity for firms to signal that their publicly traded securities are undervalued.[8] Prices of restricted stock are established through direct negotiation between the issuer and the investor. These negotiations focus on evaluating both public and private information concerning firm prospects. Costs of obtaining and evaluating target firm information, which is often proprietary, are often quite significant, and the price concession that emerges is likely to represent compensation to the long-term investor for bearing these costs. This hypothesis suggests that the discount is not due to illiquidity, but rather represents a return to the investor for the information search investment being made.

Interestingly, K. H. Wruck reports that firms placing equity privately are associated with positive abnormal returns averaging 4.4 percent around the announcement date.[9] The likely reason for this reaction is that public market participants perceive these firms to be less risky, because "expert" private investors with large research budgets would not invest in these securities unless their review of private and public information supported it. Hence, privately placed equity, while sold at some discount, also positively influences shares of the firm's publicly traded equity. This outcome, of course, suggests that placing restricted stock at a discount has a net benefit to the issuing firm and its shareholders. In their restricted stock study, Hertzel and Smith estimate an econometric model where one of the coefficients is interpreted to be a direct measure of the liquidity discount. The size of this coefficient, 13.5 percent, is statistically significant. In an update of this study by Mukesh Bajaj and others, the coefficient, while still significant, declined to 7.2 percent.[10] Despite the fact that many valuation professionals have latched onto these findings, Hertzel and Smith are not convinced that the coefficient is a measure of a liquidity discount. They state:

> *Discounts on restricted shares, though commonly characterized as "liquidity" discounts are unlikely to be due entirely to the two year restriction on resale under SEC Rule 144. Liquidity discounts of such magnitudes would provide strong incentives for firms to register their shares prior to issuing or to commit to quickly register shares after the private sale. Given the substantial resources of institutions that do not value liquidity highly such as life insurance companies and pension funds, it is not obvious that investors would require substantial liquidity discounts just for committing not to resell quickly.*[11]

Silber's restricted study, in contrast to those of Hertzel and Smith and Bajaj, does not estimate the liquidity discount directly. Rather, he estimates an econometric model that relates the natural logarithm, ln, of the restricted equity price discount, P^r (restricted stock price at issue date) divided by P

(exchange-traded price at issue date) to a set of explanatory variables. He then simulates the model under a set of assumptions about the values of the explanatory variables and obtains various values for the discount. The model estimated by Silber follows.

Silber Cross-Section Model of Restricted Stock Discount

$\ln(P'/P) = 4.33 + 0.036 \times \ln(REV) - 0.142 \times \ln(RBT) + 0.174 \times DERN + 0.332 \times (DCUST)$
  (0.13) (0.013)*   (0.051)*   (0.108)   (0.154)*

where $R^2 = .29$
         Standard error of regression = 0.358
                              $F = 8.1$
                              * = coefficient statistically significant
         Variable names:
             REV = firm revenues
             RBT = restricted block to total shares outstanding
             DERN = dummy variable = 1 if earnings are positive, 0 otherwise
             DCUST = dummy variable = 1 if there is a customer relationship
                         between the investor and the firm issuing the restricted
                         stock, 0 otherwise
         Time interval: 1981–1988
         Data: Security Data Corporation: 69 private placements of
             common stock of publicly traded companies

The coefficients of the explanatory variables are statistically significant from zero; that is, the ratio of each coefficient to its standard error (SE, shown in parentheses) exceeds the critical t-test value of 2 except for the DERN variable, which is slightly lower. The regression model's R^2 indicates that the model explains less than the 30 percent of the variation in the discount. This means that 70 percent of the variation is not explained by the model. The relatively low explanatory power shows up in the standard errors of the coefficients. Although the coefficients are statistically significant, the true coefficients lie within very large boundaries around these estimates. This means that the size of any predicted discount from the model can vary quite widely even if a firm's revenue and percent of equity placed is fixed.

To better understand this point, we simulated the Silber model. Following Silber, we assumed that the firm in question generated $40 million in revenue, had a market capitalization of $54 million, placed restricted stock that amounts to 13 percent of common stock outstanding, and DERN and DCUST were equal to 1 and 0, respectively. We then assumed that the coefficients on the revenue and percent placement of common outstanding stock variables varied by plus or minus one standard error (SE) around their respective estimated coefficient values. The results of these simulations, shown in Table 6.2, indicate that restricted stock discounts reported by Silber can vary from a low of 14 percent to a high of 40 percent. This variation is simply a function of the wide dispersion of the estimated coefficients around their estimated mean values. It stretches credulity to think that an institutional investor planning to purchase 13 percent of the stock of a firm with a market capitalization of $54 million would require a discount as high as 40 percent simply because the stock cannot be sold for two years. Moreover, institutional purchasers typically have large and very well diversified portfolios. Purchasing 13 percent of a $54 million firm represents a very small part of their overall portfolio. Hence, in relative terms, the risk is quite small. Unless the firm issuing the restricted stock is forced to do so, it does not seem sensible that management, knowing the risks faced by institutional investors, would agree to such an arrangement. In short, the Silber results are informative and useful, but they do not measure the price of liquidity.

IS THE LIQUIDITY DISCOUNT GREATER IN A CONTROL TRANSACTION?

Silber's research supports the conclusion that the private placement discount increases with the relative size of the restricted stock placement. While it would be natural to use the model to test what the discount would be for a control transaction, say 51 percent, such a simulation would not be appropriate if the sample did not include observations that included control transactions.[12] Since Silber's sample did not include control transactions, we need to look to other research as a guide to what a liquidity discount might be for a control transaction.

John Koeplin and others, hereafter referred to as Koeplin, have addressed this question. Koeplin notes:

TABLE 6.2 Restricted Stock Discounts under Varying Assumptions about the Size of Coefficients of the Silber Model

Percent Restricted Stock	Revenue		
	Mean − 1SE	Mean Coefficient	Mean + 1SE
Mean + 1SE	22%	18%	14%
Mean	32%	28%	24%
Mean − 1SE	40%	37%	34%

TABLE 6.3   Liquidity Discounts for Control Transactions

	Private Targets		Public Targets		Discount	
	Mean	Median	Mean	Median	Mean	Median
Panel A: Domestic transactions						
Enterprise value/EBIT	11.76	8.58	16.39	12.37	28.26*	30.62*
Enterprise value/EBITDA	8.08	6.98	10.15	8.35	20.39*	18.14*
Enterprise value to book value	2.35	1.85	2.86	1.73	17.81	7
Enterprise value to sales	1.35	1.13	1.32	1.14	−2.28	0.79

*Statistically significant.

> *We further limited the sample to all transactions in which a con-*
> *trolling interest was acquired in the transaction. Next, for each of*
> *these transactions, we identified an acquisition of a public company*
> *in the same country and the same year and the same industry. ——*
> *For every acquisition of a private company, we attempted to find an*
> *acquisition of a publicly traded company in the same four digit SIC*
> *code. For 13% of the transactions, the matching firms were not in*
> *the same 4 digit SIC code.*[13]

Koeplin estimates the private firm discount as 1 − (private firm target multiple/public firm target multiple). Table 6.3 reproduces these results, indicating that private firm discounts are statistically different from zero. The average (median) discounts based on EBIT and EBITDA multiples are 28 percent (31 percent) and 20 percent (18 percent), respectively. Although the average book value multiple is statistically significant and in line with the values of the other estimated discounts, the median is very low and not statistically significant. There is no obvious reason for such a disparity. The discounts based on sales multiples are not significant, either. This suggests that, at least for these transactions, revenue differences are not a good indicator of value differences. Nevertheless, Koeplin's results, taken as a whole, suggest that liquidity discounts associated with control transactions are not likely to exceed 30 percent. Finally, Koeplin concludes:

> *One problem with our approach is that the employment contracts*
> *for the key managers may be different in an acquisition of a private*
> *company relative to that for a public company. Specifically, the*

*owners of a private company, who are likely to be senior manage-
ment of the company, may receive part of their compensation in the
form of an employment contract. To the extent that these employment contracts entail above-market compensation, the observed
private company valuations will be less than the fair market valuations, which should include any excess value associated with these
contracts. Therefore, our estimates should be considered as an
upper bound on the private company discount.*

SUMMARY AND CONCLUSIONS

In the private valuation community, the size of the liquidity discount has
been debated extensively. Estimates of the size of the discount range from 40
percent on the high side to 7.2 percent on the low side. These differences
mainly arise from the use of different research designs and differing research
assumptions made by the investigators. We have taken a different approach:
synthesizing the results that have been produced and incorporating additional research intended to anchor the various values that are often used in
private valuation settings. Our conclusions can be summed up as follows.
Using an event study methodology, we estimated the impact of liquidity on
value by measuring the extent to which the share prices of listing firms
responded to announcements that they were moving from a quasi-private-
market environment, like the OTC prior to the establishment of the Nasdaq, to the NYSE. This experiment indicated that after controlling for
influences other than the listing announcement, share prices rose by 25 percent, implying a liquidity discount of 20 percent. Part of this price rise, however, was unrelated to improved liquidity, but rather the result of information
signaling. When the impact of this effect was removed, we concluded that
the pure liquidity effect on a share of minority stock was approximately 17
percent.

While this result is approximately equal to the 13.5 percent first
reported by Herzel and Smith in their restricted stock study, we suggested
that their results are more consistent with the information signaling hypothesis than a measure of illiquidity. The reason is that the purchasers of
restricted stock are typically institutional investors with a long investment
horizon, and as such they are not likely to require a 13.5 percent discount
for being unable to sell the stock within a two-year window.

Liquidity discounts for control shares are likely to be greater than for
minority shares. Koeplin's work, taken together, supports the general view
that pure liquidity discounts for controlling interests much in excess of 30
percent do not appear to be reasonable.

Although we have not addressed the issue in the body of this chapter, our analysis also implies that shares of S corporations are likely to be less liquid than shares of C corporations. When making an S election, the firm is limited to 75 shareholders, none of which can be institutional investors. By virtue of these constraints, S shares are less liquid than C shares. Therefore, one would expect that when valuing an S corporation, the estimated liquidity discount would necessarily be larger than for an equivalent C corporation. While there is no research that might provide guidance regarding what the size of the incremental discount might be, based on the analysis presented here, it does not appear likely that the increment would exceed 5 percent. Thus, if the sale of a 100 percent stake in a private C firm commands a discount of 20 percent, the liquidity discount for an equivalent S corporation would likely be in the neighborhood of 25 percent.

CHAPTER 7

Estimating the Value of Control

In their control premium study, Houlihan Lokey Howard and Zukin define a control premium as the additional consideration that an investor would pay over a marketable minority equity value (i.e., the *Wall Street Journal* price) in order to own a controlling interest in the common stock of a company.[1] The authors further state:

> *A controlling interest is considered to have a greater value than a minority interest because of the purchaser's ability to effect changes in the overall business structure and to influence business policies. Control premiums can vary greatly. Factors affecting the magnitude of a given control premium include:*
>
> 1. *The nature and magnitude of non-operating assets.*
> 2. *The nature and magnitude of discretionary expenses.*
> 3. *The perceived quality of existing management.*
> 4. *The nature and magnitude of business opportunities, which are not currently being exploited.*
> 5. *The ability to integrate the acquiree into the acquirer's business or distribution channels.*

This definition raises several important and immediate questions about the size of the control premium and how to estimate it when valuing a private firm. This chapter addresses these and related issues. We set the stage for this discussion by reviewing research that deals with the acquisitions of private firms, and we compare the characteristics of these acquisitions with those of the public firm takeover market. The differences between private firm and public firm acquisitions are striking, particularly as they relate to the size of the takeover premiums. We extend our discussion by addressing the takeover premiums associated with family-owned businesses. We then move ahead to the more crucial issue of how to estimate the premium under two sets of circumstances: The first is measuring the value of control when the buyers and competitive sellers are known with some certainty. The second is when buyers have not declared themselves, and the valuation analyst is forced to value the firm under the assumption of a hypothetical buyer.

THE TAKEOVER MARKET FOR PRIVATELY HELD FIRMS

The volume of acquisitions involving privately held firms has increased significantly and has recently surpassed the number of publicly traded firms that have been acquired. Table 7.1 is from a study conducted by James Ang and Ninon Kohers.[2] The data indicate that between 1984 and 1996, more than 22,000 acquisitions involving privately held firms have occurred, whereas less than 9,000 mergers and acquisitions have involved public firm targets.

Table 7.1 shows the characteristics of these transactions across a number of dimensions. For acquisitions of privately held targets, cash offers predominate, with 3,973 cases compared with stock offers and mixed (stock and cash) offers, which are about equal. For public targets, cash offers are also the most prevalent; however, unlike private firm targets, mixed offers are more frequent than cash offers. The percentage of total acquisitions that are stock offers has risen in both the public and private markets, as can be seen in Table 7.1. The average size of the acquirer is larger for public targets than for private targets by at least a factor of 2, no matter how the deal was financed. Also, the size of the transactions relative to the size of the acquirer is larger for public targets than for private targets. Cross-industry deals as a percentage of transactions done are high for both private and public targets, with public targets exceeding their private target counterparts across all financing types. For example, the percentage of private deals financed with cross-industry stock is 35.62 percent, while for public targets it is 26.05 percent. Private targets are also more likely to be purchased by foreign acquirers than by domestic acquirers. For example, in 21.12 percent of the private firm acquisitions financed with cash, the acquirer was a foreign firm. The equivalent percentage for public targets is 16.15 percent. This means that foreign firms play a larger role in the private market than in the public market. As one would expect, private deals are smaller than their public firm counterparts. As an example of this size difference, the mean value of mixed financed acquisitions in the private market is $55 million, whereas for public targets the mean value is $456 million.

The acquisition premium is measured as transaction value paid for the target divided by the target's book value of equity. The authors of the study argue that this measure is used because the market value of equity prior to the transaction is not known. Of course, the problem with using this mea-

TABLE 7.1 Takeovers

Method of Payment	Private Target Takeovers			Public Target Takeovers		
	Stock	Cash	Mixed	Stock	Cash	Mixed
Total number of mergers	1,530	3,973	1,567	856	3,103	1,343
All combined			7,070			5,302
Total merger value (in $ million)	49,056.10	165,620.50	85,106.40	301,328.60	513,765.10	603,497.30
Value all combined (in $ million)			299,783			1,418,621.00
Mean acquirer market value (in $ millions)	1,032.75 (n=979)	1,145.97 (n=1,525)	519.49 (n=804)	2,109.04 (n=644)	4,193.93 (n=623)	2,594.07 (n=347)
Mean merger size relative to acquirer (%)	8.14	5.88	12.42	13.22	9.06	17.62
% of cross-industry	35.62	49.89	47.1	26.05	71.45	69.99
% of mergers with foreign acquirers	3.14	21.12	12.19	2.1	16.15	9.38
Mean transaction value (in $ million)	$32.06 ($n$=379)	$41.70 ($n$=283)	$55.12 ($n$=317)	$352.96 ($n$=737)	$165.08 ($n$=2,277)	$455.81 ($n$=1,042)
Media offer price/ BV premium	2.3	2.2	4	2	1.9	1.85
Mean target total assets (in $ million)	$128.66 ($n$=583)	$160.60 ($n$=530)	$95.67 ($n$=477)	$1,782.06 ($n$=789)	$961.85 ($n$=2,560)	$1,395.67 ($n$=1,174)
Mean acquirer total assets (in $ million)	$4,658.93 ($n$=509)	$5,320.04 ($n$=499)	$2,260.18 ($n$=417)	$10,645.46 ($n$=654)	$8,939.07 ($n$=633)	$6,980.96 ($n$=349)
Mean acquirer q	1.47 (n=141)	1.04 (n=363)	1.05 (n=157)	1.57 (n=125)	1.01 (n=298)	1.15 (n=126)
Mean two-day CAR for acquirers (%)	1.32* (n=979)	1.83* (n=1,525)	1.99* (n=804)	-1.26* (n=644)	0.06 (n=623)	0.14 (n=347)

Different data items are provided for a sample of privately held target takeovers and a sample of publicly traded target takeovers, classified by the method of payment, over the period from January 1984 to June 1996. All value-based variables are adjusted for inflation using 1995 as the base year. Stock offers are defined as transactions made solely in stock, whereas cash offers are transactions made solely in cash, or cash and debt. Mixed offers include offers consisting of both cash and stock and/or convertibles. The market values for acquiring firms are measured 11 days before the merger announcement day. The mean merger size relative to acquirer's market value and the total transaction value. The percent of cross-industry mergers refers to the percentage of all mergers in that method of payment category that involve an acquirer and a target with different two-digit SIC codes. Likewise, the percent of mergers with foreign acquirers provides the percentage of mergers, in a particular method of payment group, involving acquirers from outside the United States. The offer price/BV premium is the total transaction value paid for the target divided by the private target's book value of equity. The acquirer q is based on the Chung and Pruitt (1994) estimation. Also, the acquirer's two-day cumulative abnormal return (CAR) is measured on days 0 and 1, where day 0 is the takeover announcement day. An asterisk (*) beside the acquirer's CAR denotes significance at the 1 percent level. The numbers in parentheses reflect those cases for which a particular data item was variable. Values shown were generated from information provided by Securities Data Company and from CRSP data.

sure is that owners of private firms have quite legitimate ways to reduce the size of reported earnings and thereby lower reported book value equity. As we know, in private firms it is common for control owners to compensate themselves and family member employees well above what they could command in the market for doing the same job. High levels of discretionary expenses also characterize many private firms. These two expense categories taken together could result in significant underreporting of earnings, which means that the resulting reported book value of equity is artificially low. The authors carried out several statistical tests that indicated that a bias was not present. Hence the median premiums reported appear to represent real differences between premiums paid for public and private targets. The most striking result is that private mixed deals have a median premium, 4, that is twice as great as the premium, 1.85, for mixed public transactions. In fact, for both cash and stock, the median private premium is greater than the premium paid for public targets.

Let us review these differences in more detail. The merger premiums for both private and public firms' targets are shown in Figure 7.1. Prior to 1989, the premium differences were not significant, which supports the earlier conclusion that the premium measure used is not biased upward for private firms. However, beginning in 1989, the premiums for private firms were consistently higher than for public firms, often by a wide margin. The question is, what does this tell us? The answer might be that private firms were significantly undervalued relative to public firms' targets. Hence public firm acquirers were willing to pay more money to get access to their assets. One way to shed light on this issue is to study the stock price of acquiring firms when they announce an acquisition.

Returning to Table 7.1, the two-day CAR for acquirers of private firms is significantly positive for stock, cash, and mixed deals.[3] This indicates that even though the premiums paid for private targets are relatively higher than for public targets, public firm investors believed that the acquisitions were still positive net present value investments. Indeed, if the mean two-day CAR for private stock transactions (1.32 percent) is divided by the mean merger size relative to the acquirer for stock deals (8.14 percent), then shareholders of public bidding firms, on average, earn a 16 percent gain over the price paid for the acquisition. This is not the case for public firm acquirers that purchased public firm targets. In fact in these cases the CARs are negative and significant for stock deals and statistically insignificant for cash and mixed deals. This latter result is consistent with the voluminous research on shareholder wealth and acquisitions, which concludes that shareholders of public acquiring firms do not earn abnormal returns from public firm acquisitions.

Finally, what are the factors that appear to influence the size of the pre-

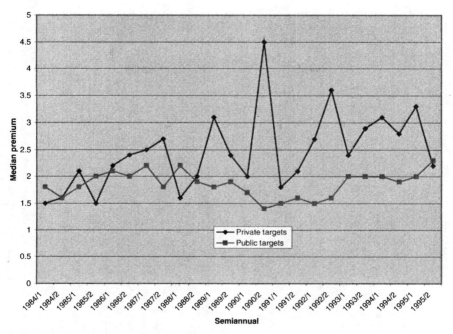

FIGURE 7.1 Private and Public Target Premiums

mium paid? Ang and Kohers estimated a regression model that attempts to isolate the various factors that influence the premium paid. The results of their analysis and the definition of the regressors are shown in Table 7.2.

Although the explanatory power of their model is low, the results are nevertheless informative. First, the FOCUS variable, which measures within industry acquisitions, is not statistically significant. This means that acquiring firms will not pay above-average premiums for private targets just because they are in the same industry. The EXCH variable indicates that the private firm premium is likely to be lower if the acquirer's stock is trading on the New York or American exchanges rather than in the Nasdaq or OTC markets. This is an important result, since it suggests that the control premium will be higher, in fact a good deal higher, if the acquirer were a private firm rather than a public firm. Why might this be the case? In many private firm transactions, the seller retains some relationship with the buyer, post-transaction. This may take the form of stock, earnout, seller loan, or an employment contract for control owners and family members. Firms that have stock trading on the NYSE are larger and less risky than firms whose equity trades on less liquid exchanges.

Therefore, sellers may be willing to accept a lower purchase price in

TABLE 7.2 Cross-Sectional Regressions: Factors Explaining the Premium for Privately Held Targets and the Market Response for Bidders

Dependent Var.	Premium Model 1		Bidder CAR Model 2		Premium Model 3		Bidder CAR Model 4	
Variables	Coeff.	t-stat	Coeff.	t-stat	Coeff.	t-stat	Coeff.	t-stat
Intercept	-0.511	(-0.06)	0.145*	(3.24)	10.93†	(1.74)	0.022	(0.748)
MV	0.682‡	(2.14)	-0.006‡	(-2.23)				
RELSIZE					0.485	(0.17)	0.098‡	(3.23)
HITEK	6.316*	(5.33)	-0.015‡	(-2.12)	5.966*	(4.93)	-0.017‡	(-2.27)
VOLUME	0.384	(0.69)	0.072‡	(2.18)	0.508	(0.94)	0.787*	(2.44)
STOCK	-0.761	(-0.66)	-0.022*	(-2.89)	-0.283	(-0.26)	-0.028*	(-4.18)
MIX	2.162†	(1.75)	-0.025*	(-3.1)	1.901	(1.59)	-0.031*	(-3.7)
FOCUS	-0.862	(-0.8)	-0.025*	(-3.58)	-0.564	(-0.54)	-0.025*	(-3.66)
EXCH	-2.365	(-2.41)	0.037*	(4.90)	-1.445†	(-1.65)	0.029*	(4.85)
ECON	-7.131	(-1.1)	0.001	(0.13)	-6.667	(-1.07)	0.024	(0.79)
F-statistic	7.53*		11.35*		6.85*		13.711*	
Obs.	677		677		677		677	
Adj. R^2	7.15%		10.88%		6.47%		13.05	

*Significant at the 0.01 level.
†Significant at the 0.10 level.
‡Significant at the 0.05 level.

The coefficients for independent variables used to explain the offer price-to-book value ratio for 677 privately held targets are provided in Models 1 and 3. In addition, the same pricing variables are used to explain the two-day cumulative abnormal returns for 677 acquirers purchasing privately held targets in Models 2 and 4. The t-values are corrected for heteroscedasticity using White's consistent estimates of the standard errors for the coefficients. The F-statistics for the overall regression models are reported as well. The offer price-to-book value, the dependent variable in Models 1 and 3, is defined as the total transaction value of a deal divided by the target's book value of equity.

In Models 2 and 4, the dependent variable is the two-day cumulative abnormal return (on day 0 and day +1) for acquirers, where day 0 is the day of announcement. The independent variables are defined as follows: MV is the log of the acquirer's market value of equity, measured 11 days prior to the takeover announcement. RELSIZE is the total transaction value divided by the sum of the acquirer's market value of equity and the transaction value. HITEK is equal to 1 for acquisitions in high-tech industries, and 0 otherwise. VOLUME refers to the total number of private target takeovers occurring in the same quarter as the private target takeover. STOCK is an indicator variable for offers financed solely with stock, while MIX is an indicator variable for mixed offers, including stock and cash and/or convertibles. FOCUS is set to 1 for takeovers in which the acquirer and target have the same two-digit SIC code. EXCH is 1 for acquiring firms trading on the NYSE or AMEX, and is 0 for Nasdaq acquiring firms. As a control variable for the economic environment at the time of the takeover, ECON is set to 1 during expansions and to 0 during recessionary periods.

exchange for contracting with a less risky buyer. Hence, under the condition that the seller is affiliated with the buying firm in some posttransaction capacity, the control premium is likely to be larger when the firm is private rather than public. The private acquiring firm will be willing to pay a higher premium because the acquiring firm believes that by agreeing to a relationship posttransaction, the seller is signaling that any inside information divulged to the buyer during the due diligence process is accurate, and therefore the business is less risky as a result.

THE TAKEOVER MARKET FOR FAMILY-OWNED BUSINESSES

To understand this issue in somewhat more detail, we now consider the motivations that owners of closely held firms have for selling. Kimberly Gleason, Anita Pennathur, and David Reeb have studied the economics of acquiring family-owned businesses.[4] The data they have compiled includes both private and public firms, and although their data set does not match the data used by Ang, family-owned public firms are likely to be far closer in structure and managerial motivation to private firms than are public firms that are not dominated by family members. Thus, this data set, despite the fact that it includes both private and public firms, can shed light on the motivation to sell closely held firms. Table 7.3 shows the characteristics of target firms in the Gleason sample, Panel A, and the selling motives for those firms for which this information was available, Panel B. Panel C provides details on the CEO's relationship to the founder for 149 firms for which such information is obtainable. Panel D provides detail on the subsequent role of the founding family in the acquired entity.

Approximately 60 percent of the sample of family-owned firms had family member ownership that was 50 percent or greater. Hence, family members controlled the bulk of the firms in the sample. Panel B shows the motives for selling. Three factors immediately stand out: (1) succession issues (17 percent), (2) growth objectives beyond the scope of the family (27 percent), and (3) desire for shareholders to diversify stake.

Panel D supports the notion that owners tend to remain with the acquired entity posttransaction in one capacity or another. In more than 40 percent of the firms in the sample, founders remain either in an executive capacity or as a board member. If this is true for a larger sample of firms, and particularly where the firms in question are private, then one would expect premiums to be larger, all else equal, for these firms than equivalent public firms.

Let us now summarize our findings and their implications for the size of the control premium. Premiums paid for private firms are greater than

TABLE 7.3 Target Characteristics

Panel A: Panel A provides details on levels of family ownership for 191 target firms for which ownership data were obtainable. Targets are both public and private firms.

Ownership Distribution	Number of Firms	% of Firms
20–29%	34	17.8
30–39%	23	12.04
40–49%	17	8.9
50–59%	37	19.37
60–69%	14	7.33
70–79%	12	6.28
80–89%	8	4.19
90–99%	5	2.62
100%	41	21.47
Total	191	100%

Panel B: Panel B provides details on motives for the sale of the family business for 123 firms where such information is obtainable. Targets are both public and private firms.

Motives for Selling Business	Number of Firms	% of Firms
Family disputes	12	9.76
Succession issues	21	17.07
Access to capital	4	3.25
Distress	17	13.82
Growth objectives beyond the scope of the family	33	26.83
Desire of shareholders to diversify stake	16	13.01
Estate taxes	4	3.25
Good deal financially	12	9.76
Career enhancement	4	3.25
Total	123	100%

Panel C: Panel C provides details on CEO's relationship to the founder for 149 firms for which such information is obtainable. Targets are both public and private firms.

Relationship to Founder	Number of Firms	% of Firms
Founder	61	40.94
Child	45	30.2
Grandchild	28	18.79
Subsequent	15	10.07
Total	149	100%

(continued)

TABLE 7.3 (Continued)

Panel D: Panel D provides detail on the subsequent role of the founding family for the 126 firms for which such information is available. Targets are both public and private firms.

Subsequent Role of Founding Family	Number of Firms	% of Firms
New executive role	35	27.78
Board member	17	13.49
Consultant	12	9.52
No role	10	7.94
Old management remains in place	36	28.57
Total	126	100%

premiums paid for equivalent public firms irrespective of how the acquisition is financed.

- Private firm premiums can be 100 percent greater than premiums paid for equivalent public firms. For example, premiums paid for private firms that were cash-financed were four times book value equity; for cash-financed acquisitions of public firms, the mean premium was twice book value.
- Acquiring public firms will on average pay less for a private firm acquisition than an acquiring private firm. This is due to the risk aversion of the seller, who is willing to accept a lower premium from a public firm that the seller views as less risky than a competitive acquiring firm that is private.
- Private firm acquirers appear to be willing to pay a higher premium than public firm acquirers when the selling control owner has a financial interest in the success of the new firm.

ESTIMATING THE CONTROL PREMIUM

Private firms are often valued for nontransaction purposes. Nontransaction valuations include valuing shares of private firms for estate planning purposes, estate tax calculations, marital dissolution, and charitable gifting. In these cases, the valuation analyst needs to estimate the size of the control premium.[5] When the buyers and sellers are known, analysts generally have sufficient information to estimate the size of the control premium with some degree of certainty. Because there is no organized market for private firms and transactions occur sporadically, it is often difficult for a valuation analyst to identify potential buyers. In these circumstances, the valuation analyst often uses the most recent mean or median from published control premium studies as the best estimate, since the information needed to obtain a more informed estimate, namely, who the buyers are, may not be available. However, as we show subsequently, defaulting to using the median control premium is likely to be inappropriate and, in general, will overstate the size of the control premium and hence the estimated control value of the private firm. In these cases, we show that the value of *pure control,* the incremental value a buyer will pay to run the firm in the same way as the seller, can be estimated using an option-pricing framework. This value will be lower than the value of control that includes an estimate of the synergy that a known buyer expects to create, posttransaction. This latter value can be estimated only if the buyers and/or their buying motivations are known with some degree of certainty. When this is not the case, there is no basis for estimating the synergy value, and, in general, a control premium that includes it will overstate the value of control in these circumstances.

The Control Premium Puzzle

In the beginning of this chapter we quoted a statement by Houlihan, Lokey, Howard, and Zukin about the factors that determine a control premium.[6] We repeat the quote here to place the issues involved in estimating the control premium in perspective:

> *A controlling interest is considered to have a greater value than a minority interest because of the purchaser's ability to effect changes in the overall business structure and to influence business policies. Control premiums can vary greatly. Factors affecting the magnitude of a given control premium include:*
>
> 1. *The nature and magnitude of non-operating assets.*
> 2. *The nature and magnitude of discretionary expenses.*
> 3. *The perceived quality of existing management.*
> 4. *The nature and magnitude of business opportunities, which are not currently being exploited.*
> 5. *The ability to integrate the acquiree into the acquirer's business or distribution channels.*

These factors fall into two broad categories:

1. Managing the cash flows and associated assets of a target business on a business-as-usual basis (items 1 to 3).
2. Putting additional assets in place to take advantage of perceived business growth opportunities that are not being exploited (items 4 and 5).

Business as usual means that management expects to run the firm in the future as it has in the past. Category 1 is distinguished from category 2 in that the former is a function of the risks and opportunities of the business only as it is currently configured. In contrast, category 2 requires the purchase of new assets to take advantage of new perceived business opportunities that have risk and opportunity profiles that are substantively different than the risks and opportunities inherent in the business-as-usual strategy. Category 2 requires new investment to take advantage of these opportunities, which emerge only if the target is acquired. Moreover, one can assess category 2 factors only if the acquiring firms and their strategies are known with some acceptable level of certainty. By contrast, category 1 risks and opportunities are known, because they are a function only of the target firm's in-place business strategies. To see the difference between the valuation implications of category 1 and category 2 factors, consider the value distribution curves in Figure 7.2.

Category 1 factors determine the shape of the distribution of possible valuation outcomes, curve A, with V_1 the median of the distribution of outcomes. For purely exposition purposes, we assume the value distribution is normal. The curve shows that a business-as-usual strategy can give rise to a multitude of valuation outcomes, although the range of outcomes is bounded. For example, the chances of a business-as-usual strategy creating a value as large as V_2* is zero. However, V_2* becomes possible if the value distribution were curve B rather than curve A. However, curve B is possible only when category 2 factors are in play. That is, category 2 factors are different in that they are a function of buyer's capacity to alter the shape and/or

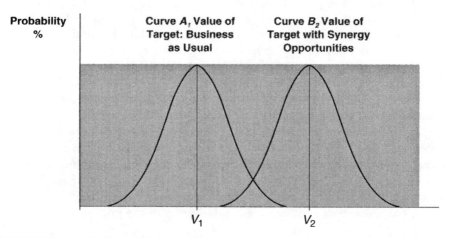

FIGURE 7.2 Target Firm Value Distribution Curves

position of the target firm's distribution of valuation outcomes. Here, the probabilities associated with different valuation outcomes are known only when both buyers declare themselves and provide sufficient data to allow one to make a judgment about various valuation outcomes. Category 2–related outcomes are not possible when the target adopts a business-as-usual strategy. They emerge only when the assets of the target and the buying firm are joined, creating the potential for new possibilities. We refer to this cojoining of assets as *synergy options*. Based on this articulation, we assert that a control premium is made up of two components: the value of pure control and the value of synergy options.

This assertion provides the logic, and as we show subsequently, the mathematics for establishing a theoretical range for the control premium. For example, if the market of buyers is made up of those who will generally manage the business in much the same way as it has been managed, then one would conclude that the control premium paid should not exceed the value of pure control. As a practical matter, market conditions at the time of the transaction will dictate whether the winning bid will include a control premium that is above or below the value of pure control. However, we would expect the average of these deviations to be zero across a sufficient number of nonsynergy transactions. We would also expect a similar outcome when the buyers have synergy options. Thus, we argue that the expected value of any control premium is equal to the expected value of pure control plus the expected value of the synergy option. Although acquirers will pay premiums outside this range, deviations should be limited by the gravitational pull of any established control premium range.

The control option-pricing framework offers several important insights into the control premium puzzle. First, the value of pure control implies that even if a buyer plans to continue a business-as-usual strategy and manages the assets in the same way as the current owner, the buyer would be willing to pay a premium over the present value of cash flows. Why? The answer is that there is always a chance that circumstances will emerge in which the value of a firm's assets will be further down the right-hand side of the value distribution. The premium paid is the cost incurred for the right to be able to capture this benefit if it occurs. Hence, one can think of a two-stage transaction process. In the first, the acquirer buys a pure control option from the seller with an exercise price equal to the minority value of the firm. The buyer retains the right to exercise the option for some predetermined period. During stage 2, the buyer decides whether to exercise or not. If the buyer exercises, then the price paid for the firm is equal to the firm's minority value, the present value of expected cash flows plus the price of the control option.

The second implication is that the value of pure control can be determined without knowing who the buyer happens to be since its value depends only on the risks and opportunities inherent in the business as usual activities of the selling firm. Third, as a practical matter, many private firm valuations are done where the buyers are not known or where their motives for purchasing are not well understood by the valuation analyst. This occurs because private firm transactions are discontinuous, and information required to understand the motives of buyers is not publicly available. Hence, the cost of acquiring this information is prohibitive. In this circumstance, any control value applied by the analyst should reflect only the value of pure control.

This last point has very practical implications for how controlling and minority interests are valued. It is quite common that when a valuation analyst is valuing a controlled transaction, the explicit premium applied is an average or the median of control values from a current control premium study.[6] Often, the valuation analyst looks for guidance from past court decisions, or perhaps the IRS has opined on an allowable control premium range. However, reliance on these sources should not provide the valuation analyst with a sense of comfort since the logic embedded in such solutions are not, except by chance, consistent with what the premium would in fact be if a transaction took place. Buyers and sellers establish these premiums based on the unique characteristics of the assets being transacted and what the buyer plans to do with the assets once owned. Hence, any estimate of what the proper control premium ought to be should be the result of quantitatively linking the risks and opportunities inherent in the transaction to the size of the expected premium paid. Defaulting to applying a median control value does not meet this standard.

The Value of Pure Control: Setting the Stage

Let us consider the case of the purchase of a local veterinary practice by a firm whose strategy is to roll up veterinary practices. The roll-up strategy is designed to create value by introducing professional management, reducing overhead costs, and significantly lowering prices for supplies when they are purchased in bulk. Finally, by having a network of veterinary practices covering a wide geographic area, customers can more easily be retained by the network even when they are lost to the local practice. Hence, revenue retention is greater and the cost of obtaining new customers for any one practice in the network is necessarily lower. Based on these facts, perhaps the value of control is worth about 20 percent or more over any reasonable estimate of the present value of the target's cash flows.

What happens if the strategic buyer decides not to buy any more practices and there are no other similar strategic buyers willing to commit funds around the valuation date? Does this mean that a veterinary practice that just comes on the market should command no control premium? The answer is that the firm's value should reflect a control premium but not the value assigned by the strategic buyer. The reason is that the owner of the firm has decided to deploy the assets of the firm in a certain way in order to achieve the firm's current cash flow status. The control owner has the right to change the way the firm's assets are deployed and can do this at his or her discretion. This is what is meant by *control:* having the right to change the way the assets of the firm are used and/or financed. This right has value no matter who the potential buyer is.

To see these points more clearly, let us consider the following hypothetical. Let us assume the control owner has a portfolio that is made up of the value of the cash flows from current assets and a control option on these assets. The owner desires to sell the business and the buyer indicates she is willing to purchase it at a price equal to the sum of the present value of the expected cash flows, although the buyer needs some additional time to evaluate whether the firm has additional cash flow potential that is not reflected in the selling price. The seller indicates that he will sell the buyer a call option on the firm with an exercise price equal to the present value of expected cash flows. The option can be exercised at any time over the course of the next 12 months. The buyer agrees and subsequently exercises the option and purchases the firm. The purchase price, which is the firm's control value, is then equal to the present value of the expected cash flows plus the price of the call option. In this setting, the present value of expected cash flows is equivalent to a firm's minority value since this is what a rational investor would pay for these cash flows. The call option is exercised when the buyer believes that current owner will not be able to deliver the expected cash flows that are the basis for determining the firm's minority value. Thus, the call price reflects the value the buyer places on control. The seller, on the other hand, receives incremental cash equal to the price of the control option prior to the sale of the firm.

Before we turn to the issue of how much above the pure control value a potential buyer might be willing to pay (i.e., the value we term the *synergy option*), let us consider the issue of pure control from another perspective. Let us assume that a recent veterinary school graduate desired to purchase only the cash flow of the veterinary practice. The current owner retained control and agreed to remain and carry on his veterinarian duties in return for receiving a market wage. In return for a one-time payment of $100, the owner agreed to distribute the cash flow of the practice to the veterinary graduate in perpetuity. This arrangement is certainly a cheaper alternative than buying a call option and then exercising it, since this strategy would cost $100 plus the price of the call. But is it? What if one day the control owner decided to increase his salary such that there was no cash flow to distribute to the recent graduate? What recourse would the graduate have? The answer is clearly none. Hence, the recent graduate who wanted to purchase the veterinary practice would pay more than $100 for the practice to ensure that she has sufficient control of the firm's assets and the cash flows they generate. The value of pure control is equivalent to an insurance policy that pays off when the control owner fails to deliver the promised cash flows. The seller would accept $100 today and a promise to deliver future cash flows to the buyer or to charge the buyer an increment over the $100 that would convert this promise to a contractual guarantee to turn control over to the buyer if the seller directed cash flow payments to himself that violated specific agreed-upon guidelines. A rational seller would certainly charge the buyer something for this guarantee, and a rational buyer would pay it.

The Synergy Control Option

The synergy control option emerges when a potential control buyer expects to deploy the assets of the target firm in a way that attempts to exploit new business opportunities and/or integrate the target's assets with those of the acquirer to obtain cash flow benefits that were not possible in the absence of the combination. This incremental cash flow results in a greater value for the control buyer, and thus she is willing to pay a premium above the value of pure control because the expected value possibilities are now far greater than they were when the business was a stand-alone operation.

To see why this is so, let us return to the veterinary practice example and assume that a strategic buyer who owns several upscale veterinary practices that are advertised as "dog hotels" is interested in purchasing the practice. The current owner houses and cares for dogs in the traditional way. The buyer believes that by combining the target practice with those that the strategic buyer already owns will enable her to reduce the costs of operating the target practice as well as raise prices for additional services offered by the dog hotel. The cost synergies emerge because redundant costs can be removed when the firms are combined that could not be when the target was a stand-alone. Such cost savings include administrative costs and purchasing necessary supplies at lower unit prices due to the fact that a larger entity can purchase in bulk and receive discounts that a smaller operation cannot. The cost of capital will also likely be lower because a larger firm is likely to be a better credit risk than a smaller firm. In addition, creating a more upscale image will allow the strategic owner to raise prices for traditional services, which will be produced at lower costs. Profit margins will expand, and expected cash flows will increase. Aggregating the benefits of the combination, the synergy buyer believes that the firm with expected synergies could be worth as much as $200. Remember that the present value of the veterinary practice's cash flows under current management is worth only $100. To generate as much as an additional $100, the new buyer estimates that an additional $50 of investment would be required. As we show next, this synergy investment can be valued as a call option on additional firm assets.

For argument's sake, let us assume that the synergy and pure control options are worth $14 and $11, respectively. What is the minimum control value the target will accept and the maximum control value the strategic buyer would be willing to pay? The minimum control value is the value of the pure control option: $11. The maximum control value is $25, of which $11 is the value of pure control and $14 is the value of the synergy option. As a practical matter, how much the strategic buyer will actually pay depends on the acquirer's bargaining power relative to the bargaining power of the target. What we know from recent studies of private firm acquisitions by public firms is that private firm targets generally have less bargaining power than their public firm acquirers.[7] This means that private firms appear to be receiving less then they might and public firms are retaining more of the expected wealth creation that occurs as a result of the acquisition.

The Option Pricing Model

In this section, we use the non-dividend-paying version of the Black-Scholes option pricing model to value each of the components of the control premium. Equation 7.1 shows the basic equations.

$$\text{TCP} = \text{CP}_p + \text{CP}_s$$

$$\text{CP}_j = V_0 \times N(d_1) - X \times e^{-rT} \times N(d_2)$$

$$j = p,s$$

$$d_1 = (\ln(V_0/X) + (r + \sigma^2/2) \times T)/\sigma \times T^{0.5}$$

$$d_2 = d_1 - \sigma \times T^{0.5}$$

$$N(d_i) = (1/(2\pi^{0.5})) \int_{-\infty}^{d_i} e^{-X^2/2} \, dX, \ i = 1,2$$

(7.1)

where   TCP = the total value of control
              CP_p = the value of pure control
              CP_s = the value of the synergy control option, or the value of a call option on additional assets needed to execute the acquirer's strategy
              V_0 = the value of the target firm's cash flows as a stand-alone entity

T = time to expiration of the option (which varies with the type of option being considered)

r = the risk-free interest rate with a duration equal to T

e^{-rT} = the discount factor based on continuous compounding

X = the exercise price (for CP_p it is equal to V_0; for CP_s it is equal to the investment required to create the synergy value)

σ = the standard deviation of returns (for CP_p it is equal to the standard deviation of returns on firm equity prior to the acquisition; for CP_s it is equal to the standard deviation of returns on equivalent synergy investments)

$N(d_i)$, $i = 1,2$ is the cumulative probability density function

Valuing the Pure Control Option As we demonstrate here, the value of an option increases with time to expiration and volatility of returns on the underlying assets. The reasoning is as follows: The longer the time to expiration of the option, the more time there is for the value of the underlying assets to exceed the purchase, or exercise, price. The greater the volatility of the returns on the firm's assets, the greater the potential of asset returns being high, resulting in the market value of the underlying assets exceeding the exercise price. Since volatility is symmetric, the market value can also be below the exercise price. However, in this case the option would not be exercised, and the transaction would not take place.

The time to expiration defines the life of the option. In the case of the pure control option, one can think of time to expiration as the due diligence period at the end of which the prospective buyer either exercises the option and buys the firm or not. Due diligence time frames vary, but they generally do not take longer than six months, although there are cases where they extend beyond a year. Table 7.4 assumes that the maximum life of a pure

TABLE 7.4 Value of Pure Control Premium Expressed as a Percent of the Stock Price Prior to the Acquisition Announcement

Assumptions: **Exercise price and market value are $100; risk-free rate = 2%.**

Time to Expiration: Months	Standard Deviations of Returns			
	25%	50%	75%	100%
3	5.19%	10.10%	14.98%	19.81%
6	7.46	14.36	21.16	27.81
9	9.25	17.64	25.85	33.78
12	10.79	20.41	29.74	38.66

control option is 12 months. The measure of volatility required by option pricing models is the standard deviation of asset returns. An approximation to calculating the volatility of private firm returns is described in Appendix 7A.

Table 7.4 shows that the value of the option increases with time. Option value also increases with volatility. What is the intuition here? Paying more for risk does not seem to make sense . . . but it does when you consider what a pure control option is. It is insurance against making a mistake. The greater the degree of uncertainty about receiving the promised cash flows from the control owner, the more one is willing to pay for insurance to find out whether entering into the bargain with the seller makes sense. If one were certain about receiving the promised cash flows, then there would be no reason to pay a premium for them. Thus, the value of pure control should be greater for a risky firm than for a less risky firm with the same exercise price.

Valuing the Synergy Option   A synergy option emerges when a buyer has an alternative strategy for the use of the firm's assets. That is, the strategic buyer believes his or her actions can produce more upside valuation possibilities relative to what is possible under the current regime. Since upside valuation possibilities increase, the strategic buyer can afford to pay an increment above the pure value of control. Let us return to our earlier example of the sale of the veterinary practice to a strategic buyer who desires to create the dog hotel. The present value of the veterinary practice cash flows is still $100. Based on the buyer's experience, it will take $50 of investment to create as much as $50 of additional value. If this strategic investment were initiated today, it would have a net present value of zero. But this traditional analysis does not consider the fact that there is potentially significant upside value to this strategic investment, perhaps as much as an incremental $100, instead of $50, in value. Moreover, the buyer knows that the $50 investment can be postponed to a later time, so more of the uncertainty surrounding the possibility of achieving the $100 upside could be resolved. The fact that the strategic investment can be postponed if conditions are not right has value. Like the pure control option, the value of the strategic option is based on the volatility of return and the time to expiration.

Based on past experience and other factors, the buyer expects the synergy strategy to have a volatility of 25 percent. Keep in mind that this volatility is not the return volatility associated with veterinary practice under old management, but rather the volatility of asset returns associated with the investment created by the "dog hotel" strategy. The volatilities will not necessarily be the same because the risk profiles of the cash flows from the business-as-usual strategy may be very different than the incremental cash flows produced by the dog hotel strategy. For example, if the acquiring firm management has been successful in implementing similar synergistic strategies in the past, then the return volatility will likely be lower than if the firm were implementing the strategy for the first time. But this does mean that the option is worth less, since a lower risk profile may mean that the value of expected cash flows is greater relative to the investment, and thus the investment has intrinsic value.[8] Again, these considerations are a function of a known buyer's characteristics and track record.

The final parameter is the time to expiration. Since this is a strategic option, it can be exercised anytime, and hence from this perspective alone it is quite valuable. In finance, the period over which the firm is expected to earn rates of return above its cost of capital is called the *competitive advantage period*. Given that a strategic option is being considered, the time to expiration should coincide with the length of time of the competitive advantage period. As a practical matter, the length of time of the competitive advantage varies depending on a multitude of factors, although it is often taken to be five years.[9] Based on an exercise price of $50, expected present value of cash flows of $50, volatility of 25 percent, and a five-year risk-free rate of return of 3 percent, the Black-Scholes model indicates that the strategic option is worth approximately $14.

Putting It All Together Using Equation 7.1, let us assume that the pure control premium has 12 months to expiration and a volatility of 25 percent. Therefore, the value of pure control is about $11 and the value of the synergy option is $14. Thus, the value of the total control premium is $25. In this example, the buyer of the veterinary practice would be willing to pay no more than $125 for the practice, or $25 above the present value of the veterinary practice's stand-alone cash flows. Clearly, if the buyer has significant negotiating leverage, the premium paid will be lower than 25 percent. As noted earlier, it appears that in such cases public firms purchase private firm targets. Alternatively, if the seller has leverage and the buyer believes that its future is compromised without purchase of the target, then payment in excess of 25 percent may well be possible. In this case, however, the parameters used to calculate the synergy option would be different and presumably give rise to a larger premium.

A PRELIMINARY TEST OF THE MODEL

This section reports preliminary results of testing whether there is a relationship between the value of pure control and actual control premiums paid. This test takes two forms. First, our theory suggests that the value of pure control should be no greater than the reported control premium. Hence, we want to test this hypothesis. Second, we want to test whether there is a significant correlation between the estimated values of pure control and the control premiums actually paid. If so, this would indicate, although not prove, that an option pricing model is a useful first step in estimating the proper size of the control premium in the presence of non-strategic buyers.

The initial sample included 86 firms that were acquired between 1998 and 2001. The data comes from Mergerstat/Shannon Pratt's Control Premium Study.[10] Of the thousands of transactions reported in this study, we randomly selected 86 acquisitions. For each firm in the sample, we collected end-of-month stock price data for 60 months prior to the two-month date from which the acquisition premium was calculated. From this data we calculated each stock's volatility as the variance of its monthly returns. The risk-free rate was the yield on a government security rate prevailing at the end of the month prior to the two-month window, with a maturity equal to the life of the option. The exercise price was set at the month-end price prior to the two-month acquisition window. For each firm the pure control premium was calculated assuming a one-year life. The value of the synergy option was calculated as the difference between the reported control premium and the estimated value of the pure control option. Appendix 7B contains all the data in this study. Table 7.5 summarizes the basic results for the total sample and two subsamples.

The first subsample removes firms with reported negative control premiums. A negative control premium means that the firm was bought for less than the value of its expected cash flows. Without having any additional information about the transaction, this result makes little economic sense. Therefore, we removed these firms from our sample. Sample 3, the second subsample, removes firms that had negative synergy option values. Sixteen firms fell into this category. Negative synergy option values can arise for at least two reasons. The first reason is that the pure control premium was estimated with sufficient error such that its value exceeded the reported control premium. The error can emerge for a number of reasons. These include the option life being too long (e.g., 12 months instead of 6) and the estimated volatility being too large. Another reason is that since the acquirer purchased the firm at a discount to the firm's intrinsic value, a negative synergy value implies that the acquiring firm paid less than the value of pure control. Put differently, the seller left money on the table. At this juncture, we have no way of measuring whether the negative difference is due to measurement error or inefficient pricing. However, the fact that these negative differences occur for only 16 firms, or about 20 percent of the firms in sample 2, we expect that they are not the result of measurement error, but, rather, arise because of shrewd bargaining on the part of the buyers. Nevertheless, a more intensive analysis needs to be undertaken before any definitive conclusions can be reached on this point.

TABLE 7.5 Control Premium, Value of Pure Control, and Value of Synergy as a Percent of Preannouncement Stock Price

| | Sample 1 Original Sample: 86 Firms | | | Sample 2 Sample 1 Less Firms with Negative Control Premiums: 74 Firms in Sample | | | Sample 3 Sample 2 Less Firms with Negative Estimated Synergy Value: 58 Firms in Sample | | |
	Average	Median	SD	Average	Median	SD	Average	Median	SD
Reported control premium	47	36	66	56	44	65	66	50	70
Pure control premium	22	16	18	21	15	19	17	15	13
Estimated synergy	26	18	66	36	24	64	49	34	65

SD = standard deviation.

The results shown in Table 7.5 are interesting, the aforementioned drawbacks notwithstanding.

First, the value of pure control is less than the reported control premium for 78 percent of sample 2 (58/74).

Second, the value of pure control is generally far smaller than the value of the synergy option. In 42 out of 58 cases, the synergy option value exceeds the pure control option value, and this result is significantly different than the result obtained by pure chance. In only four cases do the differences exceed 10 percent and, of these, only two exceed 20 percent. This means that in relatively few cases the pure control option value exceeds the value of the synergy option.

This result is consistent with what one would expect. The reason is that acquisitions are generally carried out for strategic reasons, irrespective of whether the combination makes economic sense to stock market investors, and not because the acquirer simply wants to operate the target in the same way in the future as it has been run in the past. Even in cases where the chief motivation for the acquisition is to end noneconomic activities carried out by current management, one would not expect the pure control option to be worth more than the synergy option, the option to end specified activities. Indeed, during the 1980s there were a number of well-publicized takeover attempts whose primary purpose was to change management precisely because it would not respond to stock market pressures to end activities that were wasting corporate resources.[12]

Overall, Table 7.5 indicates that, on average, the value of pure control is less than the synergy option value. The relative importance of the pure control option declines as we move from sample 1 to sample 3. Sample 3 indicates that, on average, the value of pure control is 17 percent of the preacquisition announcement price, which is about 26 percent of the acquisition premium. Although not shown, the coefficient of variation for both the pure control and synergy options was calculated. This metric, measured as the ratio of the standard deviation to the average, indicates that the value of the pure control option varies far less relative to its average than does the value of the synergy option. This is true for all samples, and this result is what one would expect. The reason is that the risks associated with synergy activities are likely to be far greater than running a stand-alone business, and the exercise period for implementing the synergy option will certainly be far greater than time to expiration of a pure control option. Where both factors are in play, the synergy option will generally represent the greatest percentage of the reported control premium.

Finally, we estimated a model where the reported control premium is the dependent variable and the pure control option is the independent variable. This exercise was carried out for sample 3 firms only. Table 7.6 shows the results of this analysis.

TABLE 7.6 Relationship between Reported Control Premium and the Pure Control Option

Multiple R	0.479427062
R squared	0.229850308
Adjusted R squared	0.216097634
Standard error	0.622338539
Observations	58

ANOVA

	df	SS	MS	F	Significance F
Regression	1	6.473085778	6.473086	16.71314	0.00014028
Residual	56	21.68909442	0.387305		
Total	57	28.16218019			

Variables	Coefficients	Standard Error	t-Stat	P-value	Lower 95%
Constant term	0.219780239	0.135031015	1.627628	0.109218	−0.05071921
Pure control option	2.626734985	0.642520922	4.08817	0.00014	1.339611768

The regression model indicates that there is a significant relationship between the values of the pure control option and reported control premiums. The adjusted R^2 is 22 percent, and the coefficient of the pure control option, 2.63, is statistically significant. While these results are promising and support the use of the option pricing framework when estimating the size of a control premium, much additional research needs to be done. However, these results do lend support to the view that control owners have control options that are valuable apart from the expected cash flows of their firms.

SUMMARY

This chapter reviewed research that analyzed acquisition (control) premium paid for private firms relative to those paid for public firms. In general, the results suggest that private firm control premiums are greater than those of public firms by a wide margin. The results also suggest that the private firm increment should be higher, indicating that prices paid for private firms may be too low.

The chapter then developed a control premium model based on option pricing theory. Most private firm transactions reflect a purchase by a business-as-usual buyer as opposed to a strategic acquirer. In these cases, the control value should reflect only the value of pure control. Implicitly including a synergistic component, for example, by using the median value from published control studies, creates a significant bias in the firm's control value. Second, the value of control is not represented in the expected cash flows of the stand-alone firm. While these expected cash flows represent the expected exercise of control owner options, the value of pure control represents control options not yet exercised. Hence, the pure control option has a value in excess of the firm's expected cash flows that is independent of the value that a buyer hopes to create based on expectations of combinatorial synergies. The chapter also presented some preliminary test results that indicate the value of pure control is correlated with and lower than the reported control premium. This result is consistent with the option pricing theory of control.

APPENDIX 7A: ESTIMATING PRIVATE FIRM VOLATILITY

Employing the option pricing model to estimate control premiums requires a measure of return volatility. For private firms, this volatility can be approximated using a principle result from the CAPM shown in Equation 7A.1.

$$\sigma_i^2 = b_i^2 \times \sigma_m^2 + \sigma_{ie}^2 \qquad (7A.1)$$

where σ^2 = the variance of the volatility of returns for firm i and the market portfolio m, respectively.

σ_{ie}^2 = nonsystematic risk that can be diversified away through portfolio diversification

b_i = the single-factor CAPM beta for firm i

The expected return for firm i can be estimated from the buildup method shown in Equation 7A.2.

$$k_i = k_f + \text{beta}_i \times \text{RP}_m + \text{SP}_i + \text{FSP}_i \qquad (7A.2)$$

where $\qquad\qquad k_f$ = the expected return on the risk-free asset.

RP_i, SP_i, and FSP_i = risk premiums that reflect market risk, size risk, and firm-specific risk, respectively.

beta_i = the CAPM beta adjusted for size and firm-specific risk (this beta is defined as $(k_i - k_f)/\text{RP}_m$)

Equation 7A.2 can now be solved for beta_i, as shown in Equation 7A.3.

$$\text{beta}_i = (k_i - k_f)/\,\text{RP}_m - \text{SP}_i/\,\text{RP}_m - \text{FSP}_i/\text{RP}_m \qquad (7A.3)$$

The beta calculated using Equation 7A.3 is the unlevered beta adjusted for nonsystematic risk factors. If the private firm has an optimal capital structure that includes debt, the beta calculated using Equation 7A.3 must be further adjusted to reflect this risk using the well-known Hamada relationship described in Chapter 5. By substituting beta_i for b_i in Equation 7A.1, we can now approximate σ_i^2 under the assumption that σ_{ie}^2 is small or close to zero. Since the two critical nonsystematic risk factors determining a firm's risk are now incorporated into the adjusted beta, it is reasonable to assume that diversifiable risk is relatively low.

TABLE 7B.1 The Data

Target Ticker Symbol	Two-Month Premium	Date Announced	Days Prior	Stock Price	Exercise Price (Stock Price)	Volatility (Standard Deviation of Return)	Risk-Free Rate	Time Until Option Expiration (in Years)	Option Value	Option Value/ Stock Price
PDM	0.059	2/1/02	60	31.82	31.82	0.23884339	0.0216	1	3.34	0.105
LEVL	0.811	3/4/99	60	37.4375	37.4375	0.49455878	0.047	1	8.04	0.215
WLL	0.755	11/13/00	60	27.68	27.68	0.24003401	0.0609	1	3.47	0.125
RRI	0.338	7/12/99	60	16.87	16.87	0.16251598	0.0503	1	1.53	0.091
FFWD	0.411	12/17/98	60	13.75	13.75	0.40399322	0.0452	1	2.47	0.180
HOVB	−0.039	1/26/00	60	15.16666	15.16666	0.16063547	0.0612	1	1.46	0.096
DEX	0.188	7/9/00	60				0.0608	1	#DIV/0!	#DIV/0!
HRBC	−0.146	4/5/00	60	22.4375	22.4375	0.92696737	0.0615	1	8.46	0.377
JPR	0.147	3/4/02	60	22.76	22.76	0.16387286	0.0223	1	1.73	0.076
FCNB	0.853	7/27/00	60	13.3125	13.3125	0.29839351	0.0608	1	1.96	0.147
GNCI	0.471	7/5/99	60	17.75	17.75	0.55828964	0.0503	1	4.26	0.240
IHC	0.518	5/2/02	60	31.9375	31.9375	0.10073903	0.0248	1	1.70	0.053
DI	−0.270	2/26/98	60	41.4375	41.4375	0.17801075	0.0531	1	4.06	0.098
BLCA	0.603	6/28/01	60	23.3	23.3	0.18765806	0.0358	1	2.15	0.092
FSVC	−0.072	8/17/99	60	4.3125	4.3125	0.27786143	0.052	1	0.58	0.135
AQM	1.083	6/14/99	60	3	3	0.32180806	0.051	1	0.45	0.151
GPM	0.290	11/2/00	60	3.5	3.5	0.31779238	0.0609	1	0.54	0.154
DDDP	0.907	1/16/03	60	3.08	3.08	0.1629972	0.0136	1	0.22	0.072
LJLB	0.516	6/8/00	60	8.75	8.75	1.92345225	0.0617	1	5.90	0.674
CBG	0.362	11/13/00	60	11.87	11.87	0.97908969	0.0609	1	4.68	0.395
AXPH	0.146	6/13/01	60	2.76	2.76	0.73686678	0.0358	1	0.83	0.300
CSRV	0.194	9/8/97	60				0.0552	1	#DIV/0!	#DIV/0!
CTYA	0.592	3/5/99	60	31.1875	31.1875	1.09712883	0.0478	1	13.43	0.431

EACO	0.194	7/24/01	60	1.29	1.29	0.3427552	0.0362	1	0.20	0.152
FSA	0.545	3/14/00	60	49.18	49.18	0.20692364	0.0622	1	5.59	0.114
MTRA	0.499	6/7/99	60	1.25	1.25	0.19860663	0.051	1	0.13	0.105
RATL	1.448	12/6/02	60	5.8	5.8	2.96669103	0.0145	1	5.01	0.863
EXEC	0.413	1/6/99	60	11	11	0.11174124	0.0451	1	0.76	0.069
KSTN	0.363	5/17/00	60	17.75	17.75	0.26845225	0.0633	1	2.43	0.137
OK	0.346	11/20/00	60	0.8875	0.8875	0.67249848	0.0609	1	0.25	0.286
BKC	0.414	7/19/01	60	22.35	22.35	0.2726488	0.0362	1	2.80	0.125
NEWZ	1.018	8/7/01	60	1.17	1.17	0.40310732	0.0347	1	0.20	0.175
CTG	0.063	6/30/99	60	24.06	24.06	0.0756089	0.051	1	1.46	0.061
LUSA	0.711	5/17/99	60	12.125	12.125	0.34272183	0.0485	1	1.91	0.158
NRC	0.170	2/16/99	60	47.625	47.625	0.15963353	0.047	1	4.18	0.088
PATH	0.684	12/9/02	60	13.01	13.01	0.82039827	0.0145	1	4.21	0.323
RELY	0.140	8/30/99	60	29	29	0.32318868	0.052	1	4.41	0.152
PRFC	0.295	6/14/01	60			0.35261924	0.0358	1	#DIV/0!	#DIV/0!
MWFD	0.430	11/12/97	60	21.75	21.75	0.57958798	0.0546	1	3.58	0.164
VLP	0.217	8/29/97	60	13.125	13.125	0.40532011	0.0556	1	3.28	0.250
NEWI	0.048	7/14/98	60			0.51928943	0.0536	1	#DIV/0!	#DIV/0!
RCHY	0.400	10/1/98	60	6.75	6.75	0.40927142	0.0471	1	1.22	0.181
CMSS	1.386	1/30/01	60	2.25	2.25	0.54406892	0.0481	1	0.50	0.224
EFS	-0.024	11/14/00	60	14.37	14.37	0.35905307	0.0609	1	2.71	0.189
IPSW	0.550	2/27/02	60	13	13	0.86088897	0.0223	1	2.90	0.223
QHGI	0.241	10/19/00	60	12.62	12.62	0.16731963	0.0601	1	2.14	0.169
SBRG	1.006	11/19/01	60	2.435	2.435	0.15000739	0.0218	1	0.83	0.340
ANI	0.441	6/8/98	60			0.45564328	0.0541	1	#DIV/0!	#DIV/0!
OHSL	0.469	8/3/99	60	15	15	0.91635736	0.052	1	1.40	0.093
UWR	0.637	8/23/99	60	21.6875	21.6875	0.52754077	0.052	1	1.89	0.087
RCA	-0.191	2/18/97	60			0.09126505	0.0553	1	#DIV/0!	#DIV/0!
DS	-0.239	1/29/01	60	29.62	29.62	16.5652361	0.0481	1	5.94	0.200
SFAM	0.248	8/12/02	60	4.45	4.45		0.0176	1	1.60	0.359
IFRS	0.957	4/15/02	60	0.69	0.69		0.0248	1	0.15	0.218
PBSC	0.236	7/16/01	60	6.5	6.5		0.0362	1	0.37	0.056
IHF	0.457	6/23/00	60	14.5625	14.5625		0.0617	1	14.56	1.000

(continued)

TABLE 7B.1 (Continued)

Target Ticker Symbol	Two-Month Premium	Date Announced	Days Prior	Stock Price	Exercise Price (Stock Price)	Volatility (Standard Deviation of Return)	Risk-Free Rate	Time Until Option Expiration (in Years)	Option Value	Option Value/Stock Price
CLMT	1.042	4/9/98	60	13.125	13.125	0.15582329	0.0538	1	1.18	0.090
FBCG	0.020	12/15/99	60	19.5	19.5	0.36568767	0.0584	1	3.34	0.171
QDEK	0.040	10/15/98	60	0.40625	0.40625	3.25058746	0.0412	1	0.36	0.898
COHB	0.228	11/24/00	60	17.12	17.12	0.15398899	0.0609	1	1.60	0.094
ASTX	-0.217	10/2/00	60	17.625	17.625	1.05084938	0.0613	1	7.39	0.419
EFBI	0.792	9/25/98	60	28.25	28.25	0.4146943	0.0471	1	5.21	0.185
BKTI	0.578	8/31/01	60	19.125	19.125	0.16801242	0.0347	1	1.61	0.084
GLBN	-0.357	6/15/01	60	3.544653	3.544653	1.21826585	0.0358	1	1.66	0.467
FMY	0.316	10/19/98	60	40.375	40.375	0.52161512	0.0412	1	8.98	0.222
HSTC	0.410	5/1/02	60				0.0248	1	#DIV/0!	#DIV/0!
EFIC	0.455	3/20/00	60	1	1	0.43917208	0.0622	1	0.20	0.200
FFOH	0.363	8/16/99	60	12	12	0.31768193	0.052	1	1.80	0.150
AVEI	0.504	11/30/98	60	36	36	1.62545249	0.0453	1	21.35	0.593
ILRN	3.339	1/31/01	60				0.0481	1	#DIV/0!	#DIV/0!
DEPO	0.475	10/19/98	60	1.3125	1.3125	0.33522031	0.0412	1	0.20	0.152
NRL	0.110	3/25/99	60	17.25	17.25	0.55650696	0.0478	1	4.11	0.238
DEFI	0.357	1/8/99	60	6.625	6.625	0.17234235	0.0451	1	0.61	0.091
PZL	0.600	3/25/02	60	13.75	13.75	0.3723601	0.0257	1	2.18	0.159
OEI	-0.455	11/25/98	60	14.37	14.37	1.07519989	0.0453	1	6.07	0.423
SNAP	0.152	11/21/02	60	4.98	4.98	0.31386731	0.0149	1	0.65	0.131
FCBH	5.188	5/22/01	60	0.11	0.11	1.40662754	0.0378	1	0.06	0.527
XLSW	0.300	8/18/99	60	27.75	27.75	0.3547328	0.052	1	4.55	0.164
FFA	0.073	3/30/01	60	22.65	22.65	0.11860251	0.043	1	1.59	0.070
SPYG	0.035	3/26/00	60	37.25	37.25	0.79229181	0.0622	1	12.28	0.330
CKC	0.067	1/12/01	60	10.3	10.3	0.33338745	0.0481	1	1.59	0.154
MBNY	0.301	9/6/00	60	17	17	0.40144052	0.0613	1	3.16	0.186
IGTI	1.590	6/1/00	60	0.625	0.625	0.14718605	0.0633	1	0.06	0.093

Taxes and Firm Value

Income and capital gains taxes impact the value of both private and public firms. Tax regimes influence valuation through income taxes at the business entity level, additional taxes on dividends paid to shareholders of C corporations, and capital gains taxes at both the entity level and shareholder level when a firm is transacted. The impact of taxes on the value of an S corporation remains a highly contentious topic.[1] While the tax courts appear to have concluded, at least temporarily, that pass-through entities like S corporations have an added valuation benefit because the proceeds are taxed only once at the shareholder level, this conclusion could change at any moment, although the argument for upholding it suggests that if it is overturned, it will not happen any time soon.[2]

This chapter isolates how tax regimes influence the value of private firms. In particular, we show that S corporations are more valuable than equivalent C corporations. This is true for two reasons. The first is that S corporation distributions flow directly to shareholders and are taxed only at the shareholder level. C corporation income is taxed at the firm level, and any subsequent shareholder distribution made from after-tax corporate income is taxed a second time at the shareholder level. The availability of higher after-tax cash flows to S shareholders relative to C shareholders makes S corporations more valuable than C corporations.

The second reason is that an S corporation can be sold for a higher price pretax than an equivalent C corporation. This occurs because the sale of an S corporation can be structured in such a way that the acquirer can obtain tax benefits related to taking greater depreciation expense on purchased assets whose values have been stepped up, or accounted for at market value, which generally exceeds the book value of purchased assets. In contrast, acquirers of freestanding C corporations cannot take advantage of the step-up because doing so triggers an immediate tax liability that exceeds the present value of tax benefits that accrue from stepping up the purchased assets to their market value. The final section of this chapter summarizes the research conducted by Merle Erickson and Shiing-wu Wang. This research empirically demonstrates that private S firms sell for higher multiples than comparable private C corporations.

This last result is important for valuing private S firms in particular and other pass-through entities in general. This empirical work makes perfectly clear that the theoretical tax advantages attributed to pass-through entities are, in fact, valuable and that acquirers are willing to pay for such favorable attributes.

DOUBLE TAXATION AND THE VALUE OF S AND C CORPORATIONS

Whether an S is worth more than a C is, in the first instance, related to whether not paying an entity-level tax has value to a buyer. All else equal, the S will be more valuable than an equivalent C, which pays taxes at the entity level and a second time at the shareholder level if shareholders receive distributions from after-tax profits. Since entity-level profits are passed through to the shareholder and taxed only once, at the shareholder level, an S has a valuable tax attribute that a C does not have and therefore should be worth more for this reason, all else equal. However, in practice many S firms pay the tax liability of shareholders, and to this extent such payments appear to be perfectly analogous to an entity-level tax paid by an equivalent C firm. Therefore, the value distinction between an S and a C due to different tax treatment is treated by most valuation professionals as a distinction without a difference. Hence, those who subscribe to this view conclude that an S is not more valuable than an equivalent C.

The following simple example shows how tax rates affect the values of equivalent C and S corporations. Equation 8.1 sets down the valuation identity that relates the value of a C to the value of an S.

$$V_s = V_c + (V_s - V_c) + \text{VTS} \qquad (8.1)$$

where V_s = value of S corporation
   V_c = Value of C corporation
   VTS = value of tax saving = (0.15 × dividends paid/C corporation cost of capital), where 0.15 is the statutory rate on dividend payouts

The value identity simply accepts that tax-effecting S pretax profits is equivalent to paying an entity-level tax on pretax profits of an equivalent C. This means that the after-tax cost of capital for the S and C are different to the extent that the entity-level and personal tax rates that shareholders face are not equal. Equation 8.2, the discounted free cash flow model, demonstrates the impact of differential tax regimes on values of C and S corporations.

$$V_i = [\{(R_i - C_i) \times (1 - t) - \text{net cap}X_i\}/(1 + k_i)]$$
$$+ [(R_i - C_i) \times (1 - t)] \times (1 + g_i)/(k_i - g_i)/(1 + k_i) \tag{8.2}$$

where
R = revenue
C = costs
$i = c,s$
k = before-tax cost of capital, and k_i is the after-tax cost of capital based on entity and personal tax rates, ET and PT, respectively.
g_i = growth rate of after-tax cash flow of C and S corporations, respectively
Net cap$X$ = net capital expenditures

Table 8.1 offers an example of how differential tax rates impact the values of Firm C, a C corporation, and Firm S, an S corporation. The table assumes that S and C are equivalent firms. Equivalency means that both firms have the same revenue, profitability, and risk. Capital expenditure levels net of depreciation are equal for both firms, and these expenditures are financed with equity only. The pretax cost of capital is 33 percent, and the after-tax cost of capital varies inversely with the assumed tax rates facing each firm.[3] Equation 8.2 is used to develop the valuations shown in the table.

Table 8.1 indicates that S is more valuable than C under all scenarios. In case 1, the value of S exceeds the value of C by the present value of the tax savings that occurs because S distributions are taxed only once. Consider case 3. Here the entity-level tax rate is lower than the personal tax rate. A priori, one would think that C has an advantage—and from a cash flow perspective it does. While C has more after-tax cash flow than S, the initial value of S still exceeds the value of C ($1,916.67 vs. $1,828.01). This difference emerges because the after-tax cost of capital for C is higher than for S, and the additional cash flow that C generates because of its lower tax rate does not offset its cost-of-capital disadvantage relative to S. This cost-of-capital effect is also present in case 2. Here, the personal tax rate is lower than the entity-level tax rate, and the S premium is lower than in case 3. The reason is that initially the value of C is greater than the value of S, $1,916.67 versus $1,828.01, which is due solely to the fact that the cost of capital is higher for S than for C. However, this difference is more than offset by the value of tax savings. Although not shown, this offset virtually goes away when the personal tax rate declines to 20 percent. The conclusion from this analysis is that S corporations are worth more than C corporations under virtually all plausible tax regimes.

The preceding conclusion is very much dependent on the size of the cost of capital under various tax regimes. What happens if the after-tax cost of capital is held constant and not allowed to vary with tax rates? Here we can say that C will be worth more relative to S according to how low the entity-

TABLE 8.1   Value of S and C under Different Tax Regimes ($g = 5\%$)

	Case 1		Case 2		Case 3	
	ET = 40% ($k = 20\%$) PT = 40% ($k = 20\%$)		ET = 40% ($k = 20\%$) PT = 30% ($k = 23.3\%$)		ET = 30% ($k = 23.3\%$) PT = 40% ($k = 20\%$)	
	C	S	C	S	C	S
Pretax profit	$500	$500	$500	$500	$500	$500
Entity-level tax	$200	$0	$200	$0	$150	$0
Shareholder tax paid by firm	$0	$200	$0	$150	$0	$200
After-tax income	$300	$300	$300	$350	$350	$300
Capital expenditures	$100	$100	$100	$100	$100	$100
Distribution to shareholders	$200	$200	$200	$250	$250	$200
Tax due on distribution	$30	$0	$30	$0	$38	$0
After-tax income to shareholders	$170	$200	$170	$250	$213	$200
Value of C	$1,917	$0	$1,917	$0	$1,828	$0
Value of tax saving if S	$150	$0	$150	$0	$161	$0
Initial value of S	$0	$1,917	$0	$1,828	$0	$1,917
Value of S minus value of C	$0	$0	$0	–$89	$0	$89
Final value of S	$0	$2,067	$0	$1,978	$0	$2,077
Final value of S less value of C		$150.00		$61.34		$249.37

level tax rate is relative to the personal tax rate. Although the result is not shown, imposing the constraint that the after-tax cost of capital is the same for C and S in case 3 results in the value of C exceeding the value of S by $172.62. In general, the value of tax saving will not offset an entity-level tax rate advantage that a C may have under the condition that the after-tax cost of capital does not vary with tax rates. However, this is not likely to be the case in the real world. Thus, under most real-world circumstances, an S will be worth more than an equivalent C.

What happens if no distribution is made and all funds are reinvested? Under the assumption that the entity and personal tax rates are equal, the value of a C and an equivalent S are equal. The reason is that C shareholders are not paying a second level of taxes, and hence the S has no tax advantage. Keep in mind that implicit in this assumption is that C and S face identical growth opportunities and after-tax earnings that are not distributed (i.e., retained earnings are used to finance investments that are designed to take advantage of these opportunities). Put differently, the expected rate of return on investments made by C and S are exactly equal. If this were not true, the value created by C and S would be different—and unrelated to any tax impact on value, as discussed next.

NON-INCOME-TAX FACTORS THAT AFFECT THE SIZE OF THE S PREMIUM

Non-income-tax factors that influence the size of the S premium include:

- Dollar value of capital expenditures.
- Capital constraints.
- Liquidity of privately held Cs versus equivalent S corporations.
- Capital gains tax on sale of the firm.
- Method of payment when the firm is sold.
- Making a 338 election.

INVESTMENT AND THE S TAX ADVANTAGE

Table 8.1 assumed that capital expenditures are constant across tax regimes. What are the valuation implications of relaxing this assumption while retaining the equivalency of the personal and the entity-level tax rates? More specifically, assume that C capital expenditures increase to $200 and S capital expenditures decline to $50. Because capital expenditures are lower for S than C, S's long-term free cash flow growth is lower, 1 percent versus 5 percent for C in this example. Table 8.2 shows that under these conditions C is worth more than S.

CAPITAL CONSTRAINTS AND THE VALUE OF C AND S

An interesting twist to the investment scenario relates to the financing of incremental investment. Let us assume that both the C and S face the same growth opportunities. To exploit these opportunities, the required amount of investment exceeds their capacity to finance them with internally generated funds. Hence, both firms need to seek outside funding. C can potentially obtain capital from multiple sources. S, on the other hand, is limited to 75 shareholders, none of whom can be institutional investors. S cannot access the capital markets, nor can it obtain equity from private equity sources or venture capital firms. It could potentially increase its debt load by borrowing money from a bank or by seeking privately placed loans with an insurance company. But this would increase S's credit risk, and potentially raise its after-tax cost of capital to the point where the expected after-tax cash flows would not fully warrant making the investment in the first place. Unlike C, S may not be able to take advantage of its growth opportunities because its access to capital is constrained. Thus, to the extent that C can finance its investment

TABLE 8.2 Values of C and S under Different Investment Paths

				C	S
Entity tax Rate	0.40	0.40			
			Revenue	$1,000.00	$1,000.00
Personal Income tax Rate	0.40	0.30			
			Costs	$500.00	$500.00
After-tax cost of capital @40%	0.20				
			Pretax profit	$500.00	$500.00
Tax on dividends	0.15				
			Entity-level tax at 40%	$200.00	$0.00
After-tax cost of capital @30%	0.23				
			Shareholder tax paid by firm	$0.00	$200.00
Growth (C)	0.05				
			After-tax income	$300.00	$300.00
Low growth (S)	0.01				
			Capital expenditures	$200.00	$50.00
			Distribution to shareholders	$100.00	$250.00
			Tax due on distribution	$15.00	$0.00
			After-tax income to shareholders	$85.00	$250.00
			Value of C	$1,833.33	
			Value of tax saving	$75.00	
			Initial value of S		$1,537.28
			Value of S – value of C		–$296.05
			Final value of S		$1,612.28

opportunities and S is capital-constrained, it follows that the value of S will be lower relative to the value of an equivalent C. Therefore, if a firm is facing significant investment opportunities, particularly if these opportunities are strategic in nature, the firm should not make an S election. Rather, it would be better served if it became a limited liability company (LLC) so it can preserve its tax pass-through status and yet still have access to multiple outside capital sources. In addition to capital constraints, private S corporations are also likely to be less liquid than equivalent C corporations, as noted in Chapter 6.

CAPITAL GAINS TAXATION AND THE VALUE OF FREESTANDING S AND C CORPORATIONS

The Tax Reform Act of 1986 removed the tax benefits associated with the sale of a freestanding C corporation. Prior to the passage of the act, the acquirer of a freestanding C corporation could step up purchased assets from their book values. Since depreciating these higher-valued assets gave rise to a higher noncash expense, which was then tax deductible, the acquiring firm could reduce its tax liability and raise its after-tax cash flow. Since the passage of the Tax Reform Act, the tax cost of obtaining the step-up in the acquisition of a freestanding C corporation is almost always greater than the tax benefit from the step-up. In contrast, the benefits from the step-up are still available when subsidiaries of a C corporation and pass-through entities such as S corporations are sold. The example that follows demonstrates that an acquirer will pay more for an S's tax benefits due to stepping up the value of acquired assets than it will for an equivalent C corporation.[4] The structure of a taxable acquisition of a C or S can be of three forms.

1. Taxable stock acquisition without a 338(h)(10) election.
2. Taxable stock acquisition with a 338(h)(10) election.
3. Taxable asset acquisition.

Section 338 of the Internal Revenue Code allows a purchaser to elect to treat a stock purchase of a freestanding C corporation as a taxable asset purchase. The acquirer can make the 338 election if it acquires at least 80 percent of the stock of the target firm within a 12-month period and does so in a taxable manner, which means that a significant amount of the transaction must be paid for with cash. The 338 election is made by the acquirer and does not require the consent of the target's shareholders, and the election must be made within 8.5 months of the acquisition.

In a taxable stock acquisition followed by a Section 338 election, the target corporation is treated, for tax purposes, as if it sold its gross (total) assets to a "new target" for the aggregate demand sale price (ADSP). The definition for ADSP follows, along with an example fact pattern that assumes a sale of a freestanding C corporation.

$$ADSP = P + L + t(ADSP - basis) \qquad (8.3)$$

where P = the price paid for the stock of the target
              L = the liabilities of the target (now assumed by the acquirer)
              t = the corporate tax rate
     Basis = the adjusted tax basis of the target's gross assets

The 338 election assumes two transactions take place. In the first, the acquirer purchases the stock of the target for $P. In the second transaction, the target's assets are sold to a phantom buyer for (ADSP$). Since the target is now a subsidiary of the acquirer, the sale of assets to the phantom buyer at a market value in excess of book value gives rise to a capital gain, which is a liability of the target firm, which is now part of the acquiring firm. This gain is taxable at the corporate income tax rate at the target firm level. Thus the price paid by the acquirer for the C is equal to the price paid for the stock plus the tax liability on the capital gain from the sale of the assets.

Although the acquirer pays the tax, it conceptually represents a tax liability incurred by the target firm. Once the asset sale is completed, the acquiring firm can take an incremental depreciation expense based on the difference between the market value of purchased assets and their book value. This higher noncash depreciation expense can now be written off against pretax income, which means that the acquiring firm's tax liability is now lower than it would be in the absence of this depreciation write-off.

TABLE 8.3 Capital Gains Tax versus Present Value of Tax Savings

Present Value of Tax Saving versus Capital Gains Tax Due Step-Up of Purchased Assets

Purchased assets	$1,400.00
Book value of purchased assets	$200.00
Capital gain	$1,200.00
Tax liability @ 35%	$420.00

Depreciation Write-Off	Annual Incremental Depreciation Expense	Annual Tax Saving	Present Value of Tax Saving
Year 1	$120.00	$42.00	$38.18
Year 2	$120.00	$42.00	$34.71
Year 3	$120.00	$42.00	$31.56
Year 4	$120.00	$42.00	$28.69
Year 5	$120.00	$42.00	$26.08
Year 6	$120.00	$42.00	$23.71
Year 7	$120.00	$42.00	$21.55
Year 8	$120.00	$42.00	$19.59
Year 9	$120.00	$42.00	$17.81
Year 10	$120.00	$42.00	$16.19
Total	$1,200.00	$420.00	$258.07

However, this benefit is almost always completely offset by the capital gain's tax liability, as shown in Table 8.3.

The tax on the capital gain is $420, which is paid when the assets are acquired. The incremental depreciation benefits accrue over time, and so the present value of these payments, $258.07, will always be less than the tax due for discount rates greater than zero. Hence, unless there are additional non-depreciation-related tax benefits that accrue to the acquirer, most acquisitions of freestanding C corporations are structured as stock purchases without a 338 election.

Like a C, a 338 election by an S corporation gives rise to a capital gain at the target firm level, but the tax liability passes through to the shareholder, and thus the target, as part of the acquirer, does not pay an entity-level tax. In short, an S will be worth more to an acquirer than a C when each transaction is structured as a stock purchase followed by a 338 election, because under this structure the C pays a tax at both the entity and shareholder levels, whereas the S is taxed only at the shareholder level.

OPTIMAL ACQUISITION STRUCTURES FOR FREESTANDING C AND S FIRMS: THE IMPACT OF THESE STRUCTURES ON PREACQUISITION PRICES

Let us now consider the following fact pattern.[5]

- TC and TS are identical C and S corporations.
- The net tax basis of each firm's assets is $200 ($400 historical cost, $200 accumulated depreciation).
- Neither firm has liabilities and no net operating loss carryforwards.
- Shareholders of TC and TS face ordinary income tax and capital gains rates of 40 percent and 20 percent, respectively. Shareholders have a net basis in their respective stock of $200.
- The fair market value of TC and TS is $900.
- TC's ordinary income tax and capital gains rate is 35 percent.
- All recaptured depreciation is taxed at the ordinary income tax rate.
- An acquirer wishes to purchase either TC or TS for $900 in a taxable stock acquisition in which the tax basis of the target's assets carries over to the acquirer.

What price will an acquirer pay for each firm and how will each transaction be structured? Table 8.4 shows three types of acquisition structures under which TS and TC can be purchased and the net after-tax cost of each to the acquirer.[6]

TS's shareholders would maximize their wealth by structuring the acquisition as an asset sale. Their after-tax cash would be $873.43. The acquirer would be willing to pay $1,091.79, so the after-tax cost of

TABLE 8.4 Acquisition Prices of Equivalent S and C Corporations

Fact Pattern

Stock purchase price	$900.00	$t_c = 35\%$
Net tax basis in assets	$200.00	$t_o = 40\%$
Historical cost	$400.00	$t_g = 20\%$
Accumulated depreciation	$200.00	$k = 10\%$
Shareholder's tax basis in target's stock	$200.00	Asset life = 10 yrs
Liabilities of target	$0.00	

	S Corporation Acquisition Structure			C Corporation Acquisition Structure		
	Taxable Stock Acquisition Without a Section 3.38(h)(10) Election	Taxable Stock Acquisition With a Section 3.38(h)(10) Election	Taxable Asset Acquisition	Taxable Stock Acquisition Without a Section 3.38 Election	Taxable Stock Acquisition With a Section 338 Election	Taxable Asset Acquisition
Purchase price	$900.00			$900.00		
Seller's indifference price[a]		$950.00				$1,091.79
Acquirer's indifference price[b]			$1,091.79		$1,276.92	
Target Corporation						
Taxable gain[c]	$0.00	$750.00	$891.79	$0.00	$1,076.92	$891.79
Tax liability[d]	$0.00	$0.00	$0.00	$0.00	$376.92	$312.13
Shareholder Effects						
Taxable gain[e]	$700.00	$750.00	$891.79	$700.00	$700.00	$579.66
Cash received	$900.00	$950.00	$1,091.79	$900.00	$900.00	$779.66
Tax liability[f]	$140.00	$190.00	$218.36	$140.00	$140.00	$115.93
After-tax cash	$760.00	$760.00	$873.43	$760.00	$760.00	$663.73

Acquirer After-Tax Cost

	1	2	3	4	5	6
Gross cost	$900.00	$950.00	$1,091.79	$900.00	$1,276.92	$1,091.79
Less tax benefits[g]	$0.00	$162.29	$191.79	$0.00	$231.60	$191.79
Net after-tax cost	$900.00	$787.71	$900.00	$900.00	$1,045.32	$900.00
Acquirer Tax Basis in						
Target's stock	$900.00	$950.00	$1,091.79	$900.00	n/a	n/a
Target's net assets	$200.00	$950.00	$1,091.79	$200.00	$1,276.92	$1,091.79

[a]The purchase price at which the seller is indifferent between making the Section 338(h)(1) election and not making the election when the purchase price is $900 (column 1) when the target is an S corporation. When the target is a C corporation, the purchase price at which the seller is indifferent between an asset sale and a taxable stock sale without a Section 338 election at a price of $900 (column 4).

[b]The purchase price at which the acquirer is indifferent between making the Section 338(h)(10) election and not making the election when the purchase price is $900 (column 1) when the target is an S corporation. When the target is a C corporation, the purchase price at which the acquirer is indifferent between an asset sale and a taxable stock sale without a Section 338 election at a price of $900 (column 4).

[c]Taxable gain at the target corporation level from the stock sale or the deemed sale of the target's assets (S corporation) or the sale of the target's assets (C corporation).

[d]Tax liability at the target corporation level on the taxable gain from the stock sale, the deemed asset sale (S corporation) or the asset sale (C corporation).

[e]Taxable gain at the target shareholder level. This gain is equivalent to the gain at the target corporation level if the target is an S corporation as the gain passes through to target shareholders. The gain retains its character as it passes through to target shareholders. If the target is a C corporation, this is the gain on the liquidation (redemption of target shares by the target) of the C corporation after the asset sale.

[f]Target shareholder tax liabilities are computed based on (e) and the nature of the gain to the target's shareholders if the target is an S corporation. If the target is a C corporation, the tax liability is the gain (e) multiplied by the capital gains tax rate.

[g]The present value of the tax savings resulting from stepping up the tax basis of the target's assets. Assuming that the step-up is amortized/depreciated straight line over a 10-year period, the applicable tax rate is 35 percent and the after-tax discount rate is 10 percent.

the acquisition would be $900. But this would not be optimal for the acquirer. The acquirer would rather purchase TS for $950, structure the acquisition as a stock purchase, and after purchasing the stock make a 338 election, since the after-tax cost would be $787.71. The actual transaction price would lie between $950 and $1,091.79, because for each dollar above $950, the cash position of TS's shareholders would exceed $760 and the after-tax cost would be more than $787.71 but less than $900.

Compare this outcome to that for TC. The optimal structure of the acquisition is a stock sale. The 338 election results in a higher after-tax cost for the acquirer than does a straight stock transaction or an asset sale. Shareholders of TC will not agree to an asset sale, because after taxes they wind up with less cash than they would under a stock or stock and a 338 election acquisition structure. Hence, TC will be sold for $900 and structured as a stock sale. In contrast, TS will be structured as a taxable stock sale with a 338 election. The transaction price will be at least $950, or $50 plus more than TC's transaction price of $900. This result reinforces the conclusion that an acquirer will pay more for an S corporation than it will for an equivalent C corporation, even under the assumption that the present value of after-tax cash flows are equal. As the earlier examples of the value of tax saving demonstrated, this is not likely to be the case. When one adds the income tax advantage of an S to its advantage when a transaction takes place, then the S premium is likely to exceed the minimum 5.56 percent [($950 ÷ $900) − 1] in the example.

TAX-FREE ACQUISITIONS OF FREESTANDING C CORPORATIONS

As is clear from the preceding discussion, the relationship between tax structures and value is quite complex. An in-depth discussion of these issues is beyond the scope of this book. However, for completeness, here is a summary of the main points that influence the structure of tax-free acquisitions and divestitures:

- The most common tax-free reorganization structures are 368(a), (b), and (c) reorganizations.
  (a) reorganizations are statutory mergers.
  (b) reorganizations require that the acquirer purchase at least 80 percent of the target's stock in exchange for the stock of the acquirer.
  (c) reorganizations require the acquisition of virtually all of the target's assets in exchange for the acquirer's stock.
- For a transaction to qualify as a tax-free reorganization it must have a sound business purpose, demonstrate a continuity of shareholder interest, and offer a plan to continue the business.

- There are benefits to tax-free structures as well as substantial nontax costs. Tax-free acquisitions involve the exchange of acquirer stock, and this gives rise to two potential costs. From the vantage point of the acquiring shareholder, using stock to make an acquisition results in dilution and may give rise to control issues. This often occurs when the target's ownership is concentrated and the value of the acquisition is large relative to the value of the acquirer preacquisition. By owning a great deal of the acquirer's stock, target shareholders are taking on risk postacquisition that they may not be able to diversify away in a timely way. This results because of limitations on how much of the stock they can sell or (want to sell) without putting significant downward pressure on the stock price.

TAX STRUCTURES AND DIVESTITURES

With some modifications, the tax structures that accompany divestitures are similar to those associated with freestanding businesses. As a general rule, divestitures are taxable events for the parent firm. In a tax-free transaction, the parent often receives illiquid stock of the acquirer that it has no interest in holding. In addition, since many divestitures are part of a strategic plan to redeploy firm assets, and buyers are often firms operating in the same industry, divesting parents would prefer to have the acquisition price paid in cash. The factors that influence the tax structure of divestitures are as follows:

- The most common divestiture structures are outright subsidiary sales, spin-offs, and equity carve-outs.
  A subsidiary sale where cash payment is a taxable transaction.
  A spin-off is a tax-free event since there is only an exchange of stock.
  An equity carve-out is also tax free, but unlike a spin-off it generates cash flow for the parent.
- A subsidiary sale can be taxed as stock sale or an asset sale. In an asset sale the assets are stepped up to market value. A stock sale accompanied by a 338 election may be preferable because it allows the step-up basis without incurring the costs associated with transferring the assets from parent/subsidiary to the buyer.
- A 338 election is wealth-maximizing when the stock and asset basis of the target subsidiary are identical and the purchase price exceeds the net asset basis. In this case the incremental cost of the step-up election is zero. This structure also makes sense when the tax basis of the target's assets is greater than the tax basis of the target's stock, although in most real-world cases these circumstances are not present.

■ The 338 election does not make sense when the parent's tax basis in the sold subsidiary stock far exceeds its tax basis in its net assets. This often occurs when the parent earlier acquired the subsidiary in a taxable stock acquisition, so the capital gain on net assets is far greater than the capital gain on the stock acquired as part of the earlier transaction.

DO ACQUISITION PRICES REFLECT THE VALUE OF TAX ATTRIBUTES?

As a theoretical matter, firms that have valuable tax attributes (e.g., S corporations and other pass through entities) should be worth more than equivalent firms that do not have these attributes. The question is whether there is sufficient empirical evidence to support these theoretical conclusions.

Merle Erickson and Shiing-wu Wang have undertaken research that addresses the issue of whether S corporations sell for higher purchase price multiples than comparable C corporations.[7] The researchers analyzed 77 matched pairs of taxable stock acquisitions of S corporations and C corporations completed during the period 1994 through 2000. Each matched pair was within the same two-digit SIC. Table 8.5 indicates that the 77 matched pairs are very similar across various financial measures. For example, Panel C indicates that the difference between the mean and median target EBITDA-to-revenue ratios for C and S firms is very small. Target revenue growth rates are also similar, with S firms having slightly higher growth than C firms. Transaction values are close, too, suggesting that size differences are not likely to bias statistical results.

The sample includes only private firms. The findings support the hypothesis that the target's organizational form does influence the acquisition's tax structure. All sample S corporation acquisitions were structured in a manner that steps up the tax basis of the target's assets, whereas none of the sample C corporation acquisitions result in a step-up. The authors also found that the purchase price multiples are higher for S corporations than they are for matched C corporation acquisitions. Table 8.6 shows that multiples are uniformly higher for S corporations than C corporations. The median S multiple is higher than the C median multiple by 14.4 percent, using the price-to-revenue ratio, to a high of 68.5 percent, using the median price-to-book-value ratio.

Erickson and Wang also estimated an econometric model where the dependent variable, the acquisition multiple, is a function of the following: organizational form (S or C), whether stock was a component of consideration, whether debt was used as part of the financing, and the growth in a firm's total assets. The results are presented in Table 8.7.

TABLE 8.5 Financial Comparison of Taxable Acquisition of C and S Corporations

Descriptive financial data for the sample of 77 S corporation acquisitions announced during 1994–2000, and the matched sample of C corporation acquisitions (amounts in $ million)

Panel A: 77 taxable stock acquisitions of S corporations

	Transaction Value	Target Book Value of Equity	Target Revenue	Target Pretax Income	Target EBITDA	Target Operating Cash Flow	Target Operating Cash Flow before Working Capital	Target EBITDA to Revenue	Target Revenue Growth
Mean	$50.31	$8.34	$48.80	$3.59	$4.92	$4.18	$4.22	14.77%	15.06%
Median	29.5	5.03	31.64	1.99	3.42	2.54	2.77	8.67%	12.08%
Standard deviation	62.32	10.69	53.14	4.98	5.91	5.54	4.66	18.96%	27.11%

Panel B: 77 taxable stocks acquisitions of C corporations

	Transaction Value	Target Book Value of Equity	Target Revenue	Target Pretax Income	Target EBITDA	Target Operating Cash Flow	Target Operating Cash Flow before Working Capital	Target EBITDA to Revenue	Target Revenue Growth
Mean	$46.24	$12.80	$62.28	$4.86	$7.67	$6.30	$7.10	14.09%	10.65%
Median	22.6	6.57	34.46	2.3	3.93	3.4	3.5	10.17%	8.80%
Standard deviation	60.8	22.82	77.48	9.3	12.61	8.71	10.61	21.09%	19.32%

(continued)

TABLE 8.5 (Continued)

Panel C: Difference in financial measures between target organizational form

	Transaction Value	Target Book Value of Equity	Target Revenue	Target Pretax Income	Target EBITDA	Target Operating Cash Flow	Target Operating Cash Flow before Working Capital	Target EBITDA to Revenue	Target Revenue Growth
Mean	$4.07	($4.46)	($13.48)	($1.27)	($2.75)	($2.12)	($2.88)	0.68%	4.41%
Median	$6.90	($1.54)	($2.82)	($0.31)	($0.51)	($0.86)	($0.73)	-1.50%	3.28%

Notes: Transaction value is the price paid for the target's stock. Target book value of equity is the book value of equity of the target in the period prior to the acquisition. Target revenue is the gross sales for the target in the year prior to the acquisition. Pretax income is income before taxes for the target in the period prior to the acquisition. Target EBITDA is the target's earnings before interest, taxes, depreciation, and amortization for the year prior to the acquisition. Target operating cash flow is the cash flow from the operations for the year prior to the acquisition. Target operating cash flows as reported in the statement of cash flows. Target operating cash flow before working capital adjustments is cash flow from operations before adjustments for changes in working capital (e.g., accounts receivable). For C corporations, we add corporate income tax expense to operating cash flows before adjusting for working capital changes. Target EBITDA to revenue is the target's EBITDA in the period prior to the acquisition divided by revenue for that same period. Target revenue growth is the percentage change in gross revenues from year −1 to year 0, where year 0 is the year prior to acquisition.

TABLE 8.6 Transaction Multiples

Comparison of purchase price multiples across target firm organizational form for 77 matched pairs of S corporation and C corporation acquisitions announced during 1994–2000

Panel A: Price-to-book multiple

	S Corporation Targets	C Corporation Targets	Difference	Matched Pair Difference
Mean	7.54	4.83	2.71*	2.45*
Median	5.19	3.08	2.11*	1.77*
% positive				65.6%*

Panel B: Price-to-revenues multiple

	S Corporation Targets	C Corporation Targets	Difference	Matched Pair Difference
Mean	1.29	1.01	0.28*	0.32*
Median	0.95	0.83	0.12*	0.26*
% positive				63.4%*

Panel C: Price-to-pretax-income multiple

	S Corporation Targets	C Corporation Targets	Difference	Matched Pair Difference
Mean	16.32	12.46	3.86*	3.47*
Median	10.91	10.35	0.56	1.89*
% positive				61.8%*

Panel D: Price-to-EBITDA multiple

	S Corporation Targets	C Corporation Targets	Difference	Matched Pair Difference
Mean	10.28	7.74	2.54*	2.75*
Median	8.83	6.22	2.61*	2.20*
% positive				63.6%*

Panel E: Price-to-cash-flows-from-operations multiple

	S Corporation Targets	C Corporation Targets	Difference	Matched Pair Difference
Mean	12.15	8.6	3.55*	4.42*
Median	10.18	6.19	3.99*	3.01*
% positive				66.0%*

Panel F: Price-to-cash-from-operations-before-working-capital-adjustments multiple

	S Corporation Targets	C Corporation Targets	Difference	Matched Pair Difference
Mean	13.16	8.21	4.95*	5.16*
Median	9.38	7.18	2.20*	2.84*
% positive				71.0%*

Notes: The target corporation's book value of equity as of the period prior to the acquisition is the denominator in the price-to-book multiple. Gross revenues is the denominator in the price-to-revenues multiple, while income before taxes (corporate) is the denominator in the price-to-pretax-income multiple. Earnings before interest, taxes, depreciation, and amortization is the denominator in the price-to-EBITDA multiple. Price-to-cash-flows-from-operations uses operating cash flows in the denominator. We add corporate income tax expense to operating cash flows for C corporation targets. Similarly, cash flows from operations before working capital adjustments is the denominator in the price-to-cash-flow-from-operations multiple. We also add corporate income tax expense to the denominator's value for C corporation targets.

*Significant at the 5 percent (10 percent) level (one-tail test).

TABLE 8.7 Acquisition Multiple Model

Estimate of the effect of target organization form, method of payment and growth on acquisition multiples for 77 S and matched C corporation acquisitions announced during 1994–2000

Independent Variable	Predicted Sign	Acquisition Multiple					
		Price to Book Value	Price to Revenue	Price to Pretax Income	Price to EBITDA	Price to Operating Cash Flow	Price to Operating Cash Flow before Working Capital
Intercept		4.35* (4.74)	1.16* (7.82)	12.36* (8.00)	6.97* (8.64)	8.71* (7.56)	8.49* (8.10)
ORGFORM	+	2.64* (2.20)	0.52* (2.61)	4.89* (2.44)	3.43* (3.19)	4.72* (3.11)	5.31* (3.82)
STOCK	+	0.66 (0.44)	−0.50† (−2.00)	−0.18 (−0.07)	−0.24 (−0.18)	−2.54 (−1.35)	1.03 (0.61)
DEBT	?	−1.47 (−0.64)	−0.25 (−0.72)	3.65 (0.93)	1.32 (0.68)	−2.09 (−0.76)	−0.05 (−0.02)
GROWTH	+	4.67* (2.30)	−0.09 (−0.25)	−1.06 (−0.32)	2.50* (1.79)	−1.51 (−0.48)	−2.22 (−0.98)
R^2		0.12	0.09	0.07	0.12	0.11	0.14
N =		107	113	100	108	98	106

Notes: The independent variables are defined as follows. ORGFORM is an indicator variable taking the value one if the target is an S corporation, zero if the target is a C corporation. STOCK is an indicator variable taking the value of one when the acquirer stock is a component of the consideration paid to the target's shareholders, zero otherwise. DEBT takes the value of one if the acquirer purchased the target with debt securities, zero otherwise. GROWTH is the percentage change in the target's total assets between year 0 and year −1, where year 0 is the year prior to the acquisition. Acquisition multiples are defined in Table 8.6.
*Significant at the 5 percent (1 percent) level (one-tail test).
†Significant at the 5 percent level (two-tail test).

The organizational form variable is the measure of the S premium. The sign on the coefficient is positive and statistically significant at the 5 percent level, indicating that one can be 95 percent certain that the organizational form coefficient is significantly different from zero. This means that when controlling for other variables that are likely to influence the acquisition multiple, an S firm will have a multiple that is significantly greater than the multiple for an equivalent C firm. This result holds irrespective of how the multiple is defined.

SUMMARY

This chapter demonstrated that theoretically freestanding S corporations are worth more than equivalent C corporations. The S value premium is a function of two factors. The first is that its pretax cash flows of S corporations are subject to only one level of taxation, while C corporations are subject to taxation at the entity and shareholder levels. The second relates to the fact that the acquirer of an S can take advantage of the tax savings produced from increased depreciation expense associated with stepping up the value of purchased assets, while the acquirer of a freestanding C corporation cannot. Research supports the theoretical conclusions and indicates that S corporations sell for higher multiples than equivalent C corporations.

APPENDIX 8A: ACQUIRERS' INDIFFERENCE PRICE EQUATIONS

Indifference acquisition price between a stock and asset transaction for TC shareholders is as follows:

$ATAX_{shareholder}$ = liquidation proceeds – tax basis
$760 = liquidation proceeds – [(liquidation proceeds – $200)20%]
$760 = liquidation proceeds – 20%liquidation proceeds + $40
$720 = 80%liquidation proceeds
Liquidation proceeds = $900   (8A.1)
Liquidation proceeds = price – tax
$900 = price – [(price – $400) × 35% + ($200 × 35%)]
$900 = .65price + $70
Price = $1,276.92

where   ATAX = target shareholder's after-tax cash
    Price = the pretax price paid to target shareholders
    Tax basis = the net asset basis of the target's assets, which is equal to the historical cost basis of the target's assets less the accumulated depreciation and amortization associated with the target's assets
    Liquidation proceeds = proceeds from liquidation
    Tax = tax

Indifference price between an asset and stock transaction for TS shareholders is as follows:

ATAX = price – tax
ATAX = price – (price – basis)tax rate
ATAX = price – [(price – historical cost)t_{cg} + (accum)t_{oi}]
$760 = price – [(price – $400)20% + ($200 × 40%)]   (8A.2)
$760 = price – 20%price + $80 – $80
$760 = 80%price
Price = $950

where   ATAX = target shareholder's after-tax cash
    Price = the pretax price paid to target shareholders
    Basis = the net asset basis of the target's assets, which is equal to the historical cost basis of the target's assets less the accumulated depreciation and amortization associated with the target's assets
    t_{cg} = capital gains tax rate
    t_{oi} = tax rate on ordinary income
    Historical cost = historical cost basis of the target's assets
    Accum = accumulated depreciation and amortization associated with the target's assets

CHAPTER 9

Valuation and Financial Reports

The Case of Measuring Goodwill Impairment

The accounting rules governing business combinations, goodwill, and intangible assets changed as a result of the Financial Accounting Standards Board (FASB) introducing Financial Accounting Standard (FAS) No. 141, *Business Combinations,* and No. 142, *Goodwill and Other Intangible Assets,* on June 30, 2001. The introduction of FAS 141 removed the use of pooling when accounting for acquisitions in favor of the purchase method. FAS 142 provides guidance for determining whether certain intangible assets and goodwill have lost market value, or in the language of the FASB have been *impaired,* subsequent to their purchase. Both 141 and 142 break new ground since they focus on the fair market values rather than on book values of acquired assets, liabilities, and goodwill.[1]

While a market value focus is embedded in the purchase method at the time the assets are acquired, FAS 142 extends the integration between book value and market value–based accounting by requiring that market valuing testing of acquired assets be carried out annually, or more frequently if conditions warrant.[2] Acquired intangible assets excluding goodwill are valued at their purchase price, and this price is considered to be equal to fair market value. Hence, their acquisition does not give rise to goodwill. By comparison, goodwill may emerge when valuing a reporting or business unit. Business units are combinations of physical assets (e.g., net working capital, plant, and equipment), intangible assets (e.g., customer lists, patents, copyrights), and a residual, which is termed *goodwill.* If the value of the reporting unit exceeds the fair market value of the assets that make it up, then the fair market value of goodwill is positive. If less, then goodwill is negative.[3]

Since the fair market value of goodwill can be measured only as a residual and cannot be measured directly, its impairment, or reduction in value, can be estimated only in steps. First, the fair market values of tangible and intangible assets of a reporting unit are calculated. These values are then aggregated and subtracted from the fair market value of the reporting unit. This difference is what FAS 142 refers to as the "implied fair value of goodwill." If this value is less than the carrying value of a reporting unit's goodwill, then there is goodwill impairment. This impairment must be deducted from the firm's net income in the year the loss is recognized. Both the carrying value of goodwill and the value of firm equity including goodwill are reduced by the amount of the impairment loss.

The introduction of FAS 141 and 142 standardizes the accounting for business combinations and valuing intangible assets acquired both as part of and outside of a business combination. At the same time, these changes introduce a series of uncertainties that are more related to valuation of business and intangible assets than they are to the rules governing the accounting for them. While the application of the fair market value standard is conceptually straightforward, its application to the measurement of impairment presents serious practical problems, such as the following:

- Should the fair market value of a reporting unit reflect a premium for control?
- Should the fair market value calculation include a marketability discount in those cases where the reporting unit no longer has equity trading in a liquid market?
- What is the appropriate discount rate to use if it is decided that fair market value is best measured by discounting expected cash flows?

The sections that follow clarify these issues by:

- Reviewing the steps that need to be taken to test for goodwill impairment and offering an example to illustrate the process.
- Demonstrating that statement guidance appears to require that valuation analysts value the reporting unit as a control transaction with appropriate adjustments for lack of liquidity and/or marketability.

TESTING FOR GOODWILL IMPAIRMENT

FAS 142 states that goodwill is measured at the "reporting unit" level. A *reporting unit* is an operating segment for which discrete financial information is available, thereby allowing segment management to review the financial and business operations of the segment.[4]

Goodwill impairment testing is done in two discrete steps:

1. The fair market value of the reporting unit is calculated. This valuation is done as of a specific date and must be repeated annually at the same time each year. The fair market value is compared to the carrying value of the reporting unit. If the fair market value is equal to or greater than the unit's carrying value, then goodwill of the reporting unit is not considered to be impaired. Thus, step 2 of the impairment test is not

necessary. Alternatively, "If the carrying amount of a reporting unit exceeds its fair value, the second step of the goodwill impairment test shall be performed to measure the amount of impairment loss, if any."[5]

2. In this step, the implied fair market value of goodwill is estimated and compared to the carrying value of goodwill for the reporting unit. If the carrying amount of goodwill exceeds its implied fair market value, an impairment loss equal to this excess is recorded. The recorded loss cannot exceed the carrying amount of goodwill. After a goodwill impairment loss is recorded, the adjusted carrying amount of goodwill becomes the new accounting basis for subsequent goodwill impairment tests.

An Example: DDS Inc.

DDS Inc. is a firm that purchases dental practices. The selling dentists stay on as professional practitioners, but all billing and purchases of supplies are done centrally. Between cost reductions and the implementation of better practice management techniques, DDS management expects to generate more profit per practice than these practices would on their own. Each practice is managed as a separate reporting unit. DDS management reviews the financial performance of each practice separately as it relates to meeting and exceeding established financial targets. In August 2001, DDS purchased the dental practice of Dr. Thomas Green. DDS paid the doctor $400,000 in cash and assumed $600,000 in liabilities.

The CFO of DDS, Mark G., wants to test the Green reporting unit for goodwill impairment as of March 31, 2002. Mark hires a valuation consultant to undertake step 1 of the impairment test. Based on this analysis, the Green reporting unit has a fair market value of $900,000. Since the fair market value of the reporting unit is less than its carrying value of $1 million, step 2 of the goodwill impairment process needs to be undertaken.

The consultant determined the fair market value of each identifiable physical and intangible asset and each identifiable liability, including any short- and long-term debt, as shown in Table 9.1. (Items with changed values are shown in bold type.)

The difference between the fair market value of the reporting unit, $900,000, and the aggregated fair market value of the identifiable assets, $800,000, is the fair market value of implied goodwill, $100,000. Alternatively, the implied goodwill of $100,000 can be calculated as the difference between the fair market value of equity (value of reporting unit less the fair market value of liabilities) and the fair market value of equity excluding goodwill (fair market value of identifiable assets less the fair market value of liabilities). The decline in the reporting unit's fair market value is a result of

TABLE 9.1 Balance Sheet for the Dr. Green Division of DDS

Assets	Fair Market Value of Asset Components at Acquisition Date	Fair Market Value of Asset Components as of March 31, 2002	Liabilities + Net Worth	Fair Market Value of Components of Liabilities + Net Worth at Acquisition Date	Fair Market Value of Components of Liabilities + Net Worth as of March 31, 2002
Current assets	$100,000	$100,000	Short-term debt	$100,000	$50,000
Net plant	350,000	$300,000	Other current liabilities	$100,000	$100,000
Net equipment	$250,000	$250,000	Long-term debt	$400,000	$400,000
Intangible asset: Customer list	$200,000	$150,000	Equity value excluding goodwill	$300,000	$250,000
Total identifiable assets	$900,000	$800,000	Total liabilities + net worth	$900,000	$800,000
Goodwill	$100,000	$100,000	Goodwill	$100,000	$100,000
Total value of operating unit	$1,000,000	$900,000	Total liabilities + net worth	$1,000,000	$900,000

impairment of the unit's nongoodwill assets. The values of net plant and the customer list were each reduced by $50,000, respectively, fully accounting for the unit's $100,000 reduction in value. The consultant's analysis indicated that the value of the customer list had declined. There was a loss of customers when a large local employer reduced its local head count by consolidating its operations to regional facilities outside the local area. The consultant also found that lower rents and a weaker local economy resulted in a reduced value for local professional practice office space.

In this example, the balance sheet as of March 31, 2002, correctly represents the market value of the business. Although the market value declined by $100,000 since the acquisition, that decline was fully accounted for by declines in value for the physical assets, office space, and an intangible asset, the customer list.

Let us now change this scenario to see how goodwill impairment could be found. Assume that the consultant determined the total value of the reporting unit to be $875,000 instead of $900,000, and that all of the other values for the physical and intangible assets are the same. Since the carrying value of goodwill is $100,000 at the acquisition date, the valuation analyst would conclude that goodwill has been impaired and that its carrying value should be reduced by $25,000. By reducing the fair market value of implied goodwill to $75,000, the balance sheet is again in line with market values. The goodwill basis for future impairment testing is established at $75,000, the new value of goodwill.

QUESTION OF VALUE

This discussion highlights two critical valuation issues that must be addressed by the valuation analyst. First, which methodology should be used to measure the value of the reporting unit, step 1 of the impairment test? Second, which methodologies should be used to estimate the fair market value of tangible and intangible assets in step 2?

Step 1: Measuring the Value of the Reporting Unit

- *Standard of value.* FAS 142 appeals to the fair market value standard. Paragraph 23 of Statement 142 statement states:

    Thus, the fair value of a reporting unit refers to the amount at which the unit as a whole could be bought or sold in a current transaction between willing parties.[6] Quoted market prices in active markets are the best evidence of fair value and shall be used as the basis for the measurement, if available. However, the market price of an individual equity security (and thus the market capitalization of a reporting unit with publicly traded equity securities) may not be representative of the fair value of the reporting unit as a whole. The quoted market price of an individual equity security, therefore, need not be the sole measurement basis of the fair value of a reporting unit.

A footnote to the preceding paragraph sheds additional light on the fair value standard. It states:

Substantial value may arise from the ability to take advantage of synergies and other benefits that flow from control over another entity. Consequently, measuring the fair value of a collection of assets and liabilities that operate together in a controlled entity is different from measuring the fair value of that entity's individual securities. An acquiring entity often is willing to pay more for equity securities that give it a controlling interest than an investor would pay for a number of equity securities representing less than a controlling interest. That control premium may cause the fair value of a reporting unit to exceed its market capitalization [emphasis mine].[7]

■ Paragraphs B152–B155 in Appendix B shed additional light on the reasoning that the board applied when considering valuing a reporting unit. B 154 states:

The Board acknowledges that the assertion in paragraph 23, that the market capitalization of a reporting unit with publicly traded equity securities may not be representative of the fair value of the reporting unit as a whole, can be viewed as inconsistent with the definition of fair value in FASB Statements No. 115, Accounting for Certain Investments in Debt and Equity Securities, and No. 133, Accounting for Derivative Instruments and Hedging Activities. Those Statements define fair value as: if a quoted market price is available, the fair value is the product of the number of trading units times that market price. However, the Board decided that measuring the fair value of an entity with a collection of assets and liabilities that operate together to produce cash flows is different from measuring the fair value of that entity's individual equity securities. That decision is supported by the fact that an entity often is willing to pay more for equity securities that give it a controlling interest than an investor would pay for a number of equity securities that represent less than a controlling interest.

The board's thinking on using market prices of minority value shares to determine value of an entity is unambiguous. One cannot use these prices by themselves. The fair market value of an entity is what a "willing" control buyer would pay and what a "willing" seller will accept.

This, of course, raises a whole set of very interesting questions. Who might the control buyer be? Is it a hypothetical control buyer or is the buyer in question the firm that actually purchased the unit? That is, is the buyer a firm just like the firm that in fact purchased the business for which the impairment testing is done? If so, should the value of the reporting unit be based on the incremental cash flows that were expected at the time of the acquisition, and, if so, are these expectations still reasonable? Again, who is to determine what is reasonable? In cases where the unit had shares trading in the market, then the investor expectations would be reflected in these prices and they could be used directly in step 1. But if market prices were not available, another method would have to be used. As described next, the FASB suggests using the discounted cash flow method. In cases where market prices are not available, the FASB suggests using the budgets of the reporting unit as a guide to estimating expected cash flows as long as these budgets are consistent with industry trends.

- B 155 presents the board's thinking on valuing a reporting unit that does not have publicly traded equity securities. In this instance, the board recommends that the discounted cash flow method be used.

The Board noted that in most instances quoted prices for a reporting unit would not be available and thus would not be used to measure the fair value of a reporting unit. The Board concluded that absent a quoted market price, a present value technique might be the best available technique to measure the fair value of a reporting unit. However, the Board agreed that this Statement should not preclude the use of valuation techniques other than a present value technique, as long as the resulting measurement is consistent with concept of fair value. That is, the valuation technique used should capture the five elements outlined in paragraph 23 of Concept Statement 7 and should result in a valuation that yields results similar to a discounted cash flows method.

- B 155 recognizes that discounted cash flow analysis requires projections of an entity's cash flows. The guideline established is that cash flows should "reflect the expectations that marketplace participants would use in their estimates of fair value whenever that information is available without undue cost and effort." The statement "does not preclude the use of an entity's own estimates, as long as there is no information indicating that marketplace participants would use different assumptions. If such information exists, the entity must adjust its assumptions to incorporate that market information."

- Based on the preceding discussion, the board has clearly concluded that value of a reporting unit is equal to its value as a stand-alone entity plus any value created by exploiting the expected synergies a control buyer might be able to create if the firm were sold.

Let us look at an example to illustrate this point. Let us say that Firm A purchased Firm B for $1,000. It paid this amount because it expected to receive $50 a year in perpetuity from the purchased assets, and Firm A's management expected to generate an additional $50 in perpetuity through a permanent reduction in Firm B's operating expenses. If Firm B's cost of capital were 10 percent, then Firm A would be willing to pay $1,000 for Firm B. This $1,000 would be the sum of $500 ($50 ÷ 0.10) for assets in place, plus an additional $500 ($50 ÷ 0.10) to obtain the "right" to implement its cost reduction strategy. On Firm A's books, the purchase of Firm B would be recorded as the fair value of assets in place of $500 plus the fair value of implied goodwill of $500.

Let us assume that over the course of the following year a weaker economy resulted in lower-than-expected cash flows from assets in place. Instead of $50, assets in place were expected to generate cash flow of $30 in perpetuity. If Firm B is still expected to produce an extra $50 a year through cost reductions, then the value of operating unit B would now be $800. Since there is a $200 reduction in the value of the B operating unit, step 2 of the goodwill impairment test is undertaken. The valuation analysis indicates that the fair market value of B's identified assets was $300 ($30 ÷ 0.10). The implied fair market value of goodwill is still $500 ($800 − $300). Hence, there is no goodwill impairment. Stand-alone assets are now worth less, and their reduction in value accounts for the full reduction in the value of operating unit B. In short, even if step 1 indicates impairment of value, it does not follow that the source of the reduction in value is the impairment of goodwill.

Now consider the circumstance where the cash flows from B emerge as expected. Assuming no change in interest rates, the value of the reporting unit must be at least $1,000. Why? A hypothetical buyer would have to pay a control premium, even if this buyer plans to run the reporting unit in the same way as existing management. The buyer pays a premium, because having the right to control how the unit's assets are deployed has a value. Put differently, a control buyer is purchasing access to expected cash flows plus a call option on yet undetermined cash flow increments. This call option has a value, even if the current owner is exploiting anticipated synergies. The FASB had this example in mind when it noted:

> *Board members noted that a valuation technique similar to that used to value the acquisition would most likely be used by the entity to determine fair value of the reporting unit. For example, if the purchase price were based on an expected cash flow model, that cash flow model and related assumptions would be used to measure the fair value of the reporting unit.*[8]

The Marketability Discount: How Big?   The FASB notes in passing that the value of a reporting unit's equity that does not trade in a liquid market will be less valuable than the equity of an identical reporting unit that does trade in such a market. As noted in Chapter 6, the decrement in a private firm's equity value relative to an identical public company counterpart is termed the *marketability* or *liquidity discount*. The size of discount depends on a number of factors, although even when these factors are controlled for, the range of acceptable values is quite wide.

This brings up an interesting problem. Consider again the example of Firm A, a private firm, acquiring Firm B, a public firm. When Firm B is part of Firm A, however, it is no longer a public company and its implied equity value (net assets) will be lower by virtue of the fact that the equity no longer trades in a liquid market. For purposes of impairment testing, should the net assets of Firm B be marked down for lack of marketability? The answer would seem to be yes. Forgetting for the moment the exact size of the discount, even if the expected cash flows at the impairment date are exactly equal to those at the time Firm B was acquired, the value of these cash flows would be worth less. The reason is that the implied equity no longer transacts in a liquid market. What this means is that when step 1 of the impairment test is undertaken, the value of the implied equity of Firm B will be below its carrying value, and step 2 of the impairment test would then need to be undertaken. When step 2 is completed, we would find that the value of net assets excluding goodwill would be worth less, but the value of goodwill would not be impaired. Note that if Firm B were a private firm this reduction in value would not emerge, since the marketability discount would already have been reflected in Firm B's purchase price.

The Cost of Capital   When the discounted cash flow method is used to value a reporting unit, the valuation professional must develop a cost of capital that reflects both business and financial risks of the reporting unit. When the unit shares the same business and financial risks of the parent, then the parent's cost of capital may be used. If, however, this is not the case, as is true in many acquisitions, then the cost of capital must be developed separately. It is certainly consistent with FAS 141 and 142 that the same logic that gave rise to the cost of capital used in the original acquisition analysis be applied for the purpose of impairment testing. Since the cost of capital at the impairment date is likely to be different, and in some cases quite different, than at the acquisition or last impairment testing date, then even if the expected cash flows have not changed, the value of the reporting unit will. If the interest rate level is significantly higher at the impairment testing date than at the acquisition or last impairment testing date, then the value of the reporting unit will be lower than the carrying value, all else equal. Again, step 2 of the impairment testing procedure will have to be undertaken. In this circumstance, we may find that the decline in the value of the reporting unit was fully accounted for by the decline in value of net assets, with the implied value of goodwill remaining unchanged.

Step 2: Measuring the Value of Tangible and Intangible Assets

Step 2 is more complex than step 1 because it requires that the fair market values of each of the identified tangible and intangible assets and liabilities of a reporting unit be estimated. In effect, step 2 requires that the balance sheet of a reporting unit be placed on a market value basis, as shown in Table 9.1. The basic fair market value accounting identity underlying this table can be stated as follows:

Value of reporting unit = value of identified assets + value of goodwill
= (value of reporting unit − value of liabilities) = (value of identified assets
− value of liabilities) + value of goodwill = fair market value of equity
= fair market value of net assets + fair market value of implied goodwill

If the fair market value of equity at the impairment testing date is below the net carrying value of the reporting unit, which is the equity value of the reporting unit including goodwill at the acquisition date, then step 2 is initiated. But as the preceding equation indicates, to do this one needs to calculate the fair market value of net assets. This requires that each asset be identified. For an asset to be recognized for impairment testing purposes, it must meet either of two criteria. The first is *separability,* which means that the asset can be separated from a collection of assets and sold separately. Tangible assets are clearly separable and can be sold or leased apart from their connection to the operating activities of the operating business. The second criterion is the *contractual-legal* standard. An asset is recognized as such when it gives rise to specified rights and other legal obligations. Licensing a technology and royalty agreements are two good examples. Clearly, recognized assets can meet both criteria.

Based on this discussion, it is clear that if step 2 of the impairment test is carried out, one must first recognize assets and then value them as stand-alone

TABLE 9.2 Guidance for Assigning Amounts to Assets and Liabilities

Asset and Liability Classes	Standard of Value
Marketable securities	Fair market value
Receivables	Present value of expected dollars received
Plant and equipment	Replacement cost or fair market value
Intangible assets	Fair market value
Nonmarketable securities	Appraised values

entities. This means that the synergy arising out of collective use of recognized assets is not valued separately but is effectively treated as part of goodwill.

Valuing Net Assets FAS 141, paragraph 37, provides guidelines for assigning values to individual assets and liabilities. The spirit and substance of paragraph 37 is that market prices, when available, should be used. Each asset, whether intangible or tangible, should be valued as if it were sold separately from the collection of assets that make up the reporting unit. Table 9.2 shows examples of the standards of value that should be applied to different asset classes.

To the extent that secondhand markets exist for the assets in question, these prices should be used. In most instances, market prices will not be available.[9] Examples of intangible assets that meet the criteria for recognition apart from goodwill follow. This list appears in paragraph A14 of FAS141.[10]

a. Marketing-related intangible assets
   (1) Trademarks, trade names ⊤
   (2) Service marks, collective marks, certification marks ⊤
   (3) Trade dress (unique color, shape, or package design) ⊤
   (4) Newspaper mastheads ⊤
   (5) Internet domain names ⊤
   (6) Non-competition agreements ⊤

b. Customer-related intangible assets
   (1) Customer lists ▲
   (2) Order or production backlog ⊤
   (3) Customer contracts and related customer relationships ⊤
   (4) Non-contractual customer relationships ▲

c. Artistic-related intangible assets
   (1) Plays, operas, ballets ⊤
   (2) Books, magazines, newspapers, other literary works ⊤

    (3) Musical works such as compositions, song lyrics, advertising jingles Ŧ
    (4) Pictures, photographs Ŧ
    (5) Video and audiovisual material, including motion pictures, music videos, television programs Ŧ

  d. Contract-based intangible assets
    (1) Licensing, royalty, standstill agreements Ŧ
    (2) Advertising, construction, management, service or supply contracts Ŧ
    (3) Lease agreements Ŧ
    (4) Construction permits Ŧ
    (5) Franchise agreements Ŧ
    (6) Operating and broadcast rights Ŧ
    (7) Use rights such as drilling, water, air, mineral, timber cutting, and route authorities Ŧ
    (8) Servicing contracts such as mortgage servicing contracts Ŧ
    (9) Employment contracts Ŧ

  e. Technology-based intangible assets
    (1) Patented technology Ŧ
    (2) Computer software and mask works Ŧ
    (3) Un-patented technology ▲
    (4) Databases, including title plants ▲
    (5) Trade secrets, such as secret formulas, processes, recipes Ŧ

SUMMARY

FAS 142 requires that goodwill emerging from acquisitions be tested to determine whether it has been impaired. Prior to FAS 142, goodwill was amortized over as many as 40 years, with the amortized amount deducted from net income. FAS 142 requires firms to effectively undertake a market test to see whether goodwill has been impaired. This test is completed in two steps. The first simply requires a revaluing of the reporting unit. If this value is equal to or greater than the unit's carrying value then goodwill has not been impaired. On the other hand, if the calculated value is less than the unit's carrying value, then step 2 must be undertaken. The purpose of step 2 is to assign the value of the reporting unit to its identified and recognized assets and liabilities. These assets are valued as stand-alone entities. The difference between the carrying value of assets (including goodwill) at the impairment valuation date and the market value of the reporting unit at the valuation date is implied goodwill. If this value is less than the carrying value of goodwill, then the difference is equal to the value of goodwill impairment loss.

The purpose of FAS 141 and FAS 142 is to provide investors with better financial information regarding the success of past acquisitions. In the process of doing this, the FASB has forced firms to deal with a number of thorny and, in some cases, unresolved valuation issues:

- Valuing the reporting unit from the perspective of hypothetical new buyer or from the perspective of the acquiring firm implementing its strategy for deploying the acquired assets.
- Applying a marketability discount to the value of a reporting unit when the unit no longer has equity trading in a liquid market.
- Estimating the proper cost of capital when the discounted cash flow approach is used to value the reporting unit.

Notes

Preface

1. See Walter L. Gross Jr. et al., *Petitioners v. Commissioner of Internal Revenue.*
2. See www.axiomvaluation.com.

CHAPTER 1   The Value of Fair Market Value

1. Revenue Ruling 59–60, Section 2.02.
2. Intrinsic value is another value standard in addition to those noted in the text. *Intrinsic value* refers to what an individual believes something is fundamentally worth. When willing and informed buyers and sellers have the same view of an item's fundamental worth, then intrinsic value and FMV are equal. In some states, the value standard used in marital dissolutions is intrinsic value and not FMV. Personal items, such as family heirlooms, have intrinsic value to family members, but they may have no value to unrelated parties. In this instance, intrinsic value exceeds FMV.
3. See the FMV definition in the text.
4. The control premium, CP, is equal to [(control value (CV) − minority value (MV)) ÷ minority value] × 100%. If control value is $150 and minority value is $100, then CP is 50%. The minority discount (MD) is equal to [(MV − CV) ÷ CV] × 100. Using these values, MD = [($100 − $150) ÷ $150] × 100% = −33%.
5. MD = [($100 − $125) ÷ $125] × 100% = −20%.

CHAPTER 2   Creating and Measuring the Value of Private Firms

1. When calculating the value of private firms, two adjustments need to be considered. The first is the discount for liquidity; the second is a premium above minority equity value to reflect the value of control. Because this chapter focuses on the MVM, discussions of the discount for lack of liquidity and control are left for subsequent chapters.
2. The concept of the optimal capital structure is applicable to C corporations. On this point see Franco Modigliani and Merton Miller, "The Cost of Capital, Corporation Finance and the Theory of Investment," *American Economic Review,* June 1958, pp. 261–297; "The Cost of Capital, Corporation Finance and the Theory of Investment: Reply," *American Economic Review,* September 1958, pp. 655–669; "Taxes and the Cost of Capital: A Correction," *American*

Economic Review, June 1963, pp. 433–443; and "Reply," *American Economic Review,* June 1965, pp. 524–527.

3. See Bernard J. Picchi, *The Structure of the Oil Industry: Past and Future* (New York: Salomon Brothers Inc., July 1985).
4. Chapter 5 addresses the effect of size on the cost of capital in considerable detail. Ibbotson Associates estimates of the impact of firm size on the cost of capital. Axiom Valuation Solutions has extended this work to firms that are much smaller than those covered by Ibbotson Associates. Based on Axiom's analysis, the cost of capital for smaller private firms is likely to be much greater than the cost of capital for the smallest Ibbotson size class.
5. Katherine Schipper and Abbie Smith, "The Effects of Recontracting on Shareholder Wealth," *Journal of Financial Economics,* 1983, pp. 437–467.
6. Katherine Schipper and Abbie Smith, "A Comparison of Equity Carve-Outs and Seasoned Equity Offerings," *Journal of Financial Economics* 15, January/February 1986, pp. 153–186.

CHAPTER 3   The Restructuring of Frier Manufacturing

1. Throughout the analysis, values shown were not adjusted for lack of marketability of Frier equity. This was done so performance comparisons with public firm peers could be easily made. The impact of marketability as the value of private firm shares is taken up in this chapter.
2. Stanley Jay Feldman and Timothy Sullivan, "The Impact of Productivity, Pricing, and Sales on Shareholder Wealth," *Data Resources Long-term Review,* Summer 1992, pp. 19–23.

CHAPTER 4   Valuation Models and Metrics: Discounted Free Cash Flow and the Method of Multiples

1. Market price is the firm's share price. If the target firm has debt outstanding, then the value of the firm would be equal to its estimated equity value using the method of multiples plus the value of its debt.
2. Founded in 1914, The Risk Management Association is a nonprofit, member-driven professional association whose sole purpose is to advance the use of sound risk principles in the financial services industry. RMA promotes an enterprise-wide approach to risk management that focuses on credit risk, market risk, and operational risk.
3. This adjustment does not mean that the tax deductibility of interest has no value. The value emerges when operating cash flows are valued using a lower cost of capital that emerges because interest expense is tax deductible, a topic addressed in the next chapter.
4. *Excess cash* is defined as cash on the balance sheet in excess of what is required to normally operate the business. As a guideline, cash on the balance sheet in excess of 2 percent of revenue is treated as excess cash. Working capital would then reflect this adjustment. Based on the nature of Tentex's business, it was determined that Tentex's business required cash in excess of the 2 percent guideline. Hence, no excess cash adjustment was made.

5. NOPAT + interest expense + depreciation − (gross investment) = free cash flow = NOPAT + interest expense + depreciation − (net capital expenditure − depreciation) = NOPAT + interest expense − net capital expenditure.

6. Sustainable competitive advantage is created when a firm can shield itself from competitive forces to some degree. Protection from competitive forces can emerge in a number of ways. A firm can achieve low-cost producer status through continuously improving firm productivity and passing on some of the cost savings to customers in the form of lower prices. Patents, of course, offer protection for a limited time frame. For private firms, sustaining customer allegiance is likely to be the best protection against market forces. Depending on the industry, customer allegiance results from providing excellent service, therefore making it difficult for competitive firms to bid these customers away. The combination of low prices, reliable products and services along with excellent customer service is likely to create sustainable competitive advantage.

7. To see this relationship, we define the growth index in revenue for industry i, geography g as GIREVi,g. If GIREVi is 1.10, industry revenue growth is 10%, GIREV is 1.05, GDP growth is 5%, and GIREVg is 2.1%, then GIREVi,g is equal to (GIREVg ÷ GIREV) × (GIREVi), or (1.021 ÷ 1.05) × (1.10), which equals 1.07 or a growth rate of 7%.

8. Any standard macroeconomic textbook covers the multiplier theory of investment.

9. In addition to a marketability adjustment, there is a question of whether the value of Tentex reflects control. To the extent it does not, a control premium must be added to the value shown. For now, we assume that value of control is in the cash flows, although in Chapter 7 we demonstrate that the value of control is separate from the value of underlying cash flows of a stand-alone business.

10. Price-to-EBITDA (earnings before interest, tax, depreciation, and amortization) multiples are often used to value a target firm. The EBITDA multiple, like the revenue multiple, is subject to less variability than the earnings multiple. However, while less easily distorted than earnings, EBITDA is still subject to some degree of manipulation.

11. The target capital structure represents the combination of debt and equity that minimizes the firm's cost of capital. Based on an analysis of Tentex's credit risk, it was determined that the 90-10 capital structure was optimal.

12. Equation 4.9 was used to solve for Tentex's revenue multiple, which was 1.31. The difference between this value and 1.36 is essentially rounding error.

13. Steven N. Kaplan and Richard Ruback, "The Market Pricing of Cash Flow Forecasts: Discounted Cash Flow vs. the Method of Comparables," *Journal of Applied Corporate Finance* 8, no. 4, Winter 1996, pp. 45–60.

14. Kaplan and Ruback, "Market Pricing," p. 45.

CHAPTER 5 Estimating the Cost of Capital

1. Ibbotson Associates, *Stocks, Bonds, Bills, and Inflation, Valuation Edition, and the Cost of Capital Yearbook*, 2004.

2. Ibbotson Associates, *Stock, Bonds, Bills and Inflation, Valuation Edition, 2004 Yearbook*, p. 115.

3. Ibbotson Associates, *Cost of Capital Yearbook,* 2004, pp. 3–55.
4. See Ibbotson Associates, *Cost of Capital Yearbook,* 2004, p. 34, for a discussion of the method used to create adjusted industry betas.
5. See www.axiomvaluation.com for data sources used to construct this data set.
6. A zero beta means that the return on debt is not correlated with the return on a diversified portfolio of financial securities. This is the typical assumption made about the debt beta. Note that to the extent the debt beta is not negative, which it might well be, assuming the debt beta of zero understates the systematic risk of a firm with debt.
7. Axiom sales size classes and Ibbotson Associates size premium data.
8. P. Gompers and J. Lerner, "Risk Reward and Private Equity Investments: The Challenge of Performance Assessment," *Journal of Private Equity* 1, pp. 5–12.
9. John Cochrane, "The Risk and Return of Venture Capital," NBER working paper 8066.
10. Edward Altman, "Predicting Financial Stress of Companies: Revisiting the Z Score and Zeta Models," working paper, July 2000.
11. For more information on the 7(a) loan program refer to www.sba.gov/financing/sbaloan/7a.html.
12. The example assumes that principle is paid at the end of the loan term. To the extent that principal is paid over the life of the loan, the market value of the debt would be greater than shown in the text.

CHAPTER 6   The Value of Liquidity: Estimating the Size of the Liquidity Discount

1. We use the terms *liquidity discount* and *marketability discount* interchangeably in this paper, as is customary in this literature.
2. Yakov Amihud and Haim Mendelson, "Asset Pricing and the Bid-Ask Spread," *Journal of Financial Economics* 17, 1986, pp. 223–249. Also, "The Effects of Beta, Bid-Ask Spread, Residual Risk and Size on Stock Returns," *Journal of Finance,* June 1989, pp. 479–486.
3. Yakov Amihud and Haim Mendelson, "Liquidity and Cost of Capital: Implications for Corporate Management," *The New Corporate Finance, Where Theory Meets Practice,* edited by Donald H. Chew Jr. (New York: McGraw-Hill, 1993), pp. 117–125.
4. Gary C. Sanger and John J. McConnell, "Stock Exchange Listings, Firm Value, and Security Market Efficiency: The Impact of NASDAQ," *Journal of Financial and Quantitative Analysis* 21, no. 1, March 1986, pp. 1–25.
5. The reason is that observing price behavior of an OTC stock at the time it moves to the NYSE is akin to a private firm today initially listing with a business broker and then subsequently listing on the NYSE. During the period prior to the Nasdaq, there was no electronic posting, no Internet, and pink sheet stocks were made available to investors only through the retail broker community. Hence, this research offers an important source of knowledge about the impact of liquidity, or lack thereof, on the prices of minority shares of quasi-private firms.
6. Richard B. Edelman and H. Kent Baker, "The Impact of Company Pre-Listing

Attributes on the Market Reaction to NYSE Listings, *Financial Review* 28, no. 3, August 1993, pp. 431–448.

7. John D. Emory Sr., F. R. Dengell III, and John D. Emory Jr., "Discounts for Lack of Marketability, Emory Pre-IPO Discount Studies 1980–2000 (As Adjusted October 10, 2002), *Business Valuation Review,* December 2002, pp. 190–193; William L. Silber, "Discounts on Restricted Stock: The Impact of Illiquidity on Stock Prices," *Financial Analysts Journal,* July, August 1991, pp. 60–64; Michael Hertzel and Richard Smith, "Market Discounts and Shareholder Gains for Placing Equity Privately," *Journal of Finance* 48, no. 2, June 1993, pp. 459–485.

8. S. C. Myers and N. S. Majluf, "Corporate Financing and Investment Decisions When the Firm Has Information That Investors Do Not Have," *Journal of Financial Economics* 13, pp. 187–221.

9. K. H. Wruck, "Equity Ownership Concentration and Firm Value: Evidence from Private Equity Financings," *Journal of Financial Economics* 23, pp. 3–28.

10. Mukesh Bajaj, David J. Denis, Stephen P. Ferris, and Atulya Sarin, "Firm Value and Marketability Discounts," *Journal of Law and Economics,* 2002.

11. Hertzel and Smith, "Market Discounts."

12. Regression coefficients are a function of sample characteristics. This means that simulating models under conditions that were not present during the estimation period will result in biased simulation results. In the case of simulating the Silber model under an assumption of a control placement, the simulated discounts would be much too large.

13. John Koeplin, Atulya Sarin, and Alan Shapiro, "The Private Company Discount," *Journal of Applied Corporate Finance* 12, no. 4, Winter 2000, pp. 94–101.

CHAPTER 7   Estimating the Value of Control

1. *Control Premium Study* (Los Angeles: Houlihan Lokey Howard and Zukin, 1995), p. 1.

2. James Ang and Ninon Kohers, "The Takeover Market for Privately Held Companies: The US Experience," *Cambridge Journal of Economics* 25, 2001, pp. 723–748.

3. CAR is the cumulative abnormal return. The abnormal return is the difference between the return earned and the expected return. The expected return is typically derived using a version of the CAPM.

4. Kimberly Gleason, Anita Pennathur, and David Reeb, "An Analysis of Mergers and Acquisitions of Family-Owned Businesses," working paper, October 2002.

5. James Ang and Ninon Kohers, "The Takeover Market for Privately Held Companies: The US Experience," *Cambridge Journal of Economics* 25, 2001, pp. 723–748. The authors state on p. 725: "Overall, our results show that, in contrast to acquisitions of publicly traded targets, acquisitions of privately held targets yield substantial gains for both bidder and target firms. Specifically, the event-period, abnormal returns for acquires of privately held targets are significantly positive, regardless of the method of payment used. Thus, takeovers of

privately held firms are, on average, perceived too be value enhancing for acquiring firms. Furthermore, private sellers also gain, as the premiums paid to private targets exceed those paid for publicly traded targets in either cash or stock offers."

6. On this point see Pratt, Reilly, and Schweihs, *Valuing a Business*, Chapter 14.

7. James Ang and Ninon Kohers, "The Takeover Market for Privately Held Companies: The US Experience," *Cambridge Journal of Economics* 25, 2001, pp. 723–748. The authors state on p. 725: "Overall, our results show that, in contrast to acquisitions of publicly traded targets. acquisitions of privately held targets yield substantial gains for both bidder and target firms. Specifically, the event-period, abnormal returns for acquires of privately held targets are significantly positive, regardless of the method of payment used. Thus, takeovers of privately held firms are, on average, perceived too be value enhancing for acquiring firms. Furthermore, private sellers also gain, as the premiums paid to private targets exceed those paid for publicly traded targets in either cash or stock offers."

8. An option has *intrinsic value* if the expected present value of the cash flows, excluding ongoing investment requirements. exceeds the present value of the investment requirements. This is termed an *in the money* call option.

9. The period over which a strategy is expected to be successful has a finite life based on the competitive nature of the business environment, technological developments, and the actions of competitive firms. Thus, there is nothing special about a five-year competitive advantage period.

10. The Mergerstat/Shannon Pratt's Control Premium Study currently contains approximately 3,450 total transactions, with more than 485 deals in business services, more than 430 deals on depository institutions, and 138 deals in the communications industry; 51 percent of the deals in the database have net sales less than $100 million, with the remainder having net sales greater than $100 million.

11. In the 1980s, T. Boone Pickens of Mesa Petroleum attempted to acquire Unocal to get access to its oil reserves and to stop the wasting of corporate resources on exploring and drilling for new oil supplies. As it turned out, drilling for oil was a negative NPV investment. T. Boone realized that if he had control of Unocal, he could stop the oil-drilling activity, which in turn would result in a windfall that in large part would provide the capital to finance the acquisition. As it turned out, Unocal management got the message. Unocal's defense in the Mesa tender offer battle resulted in a $2.2 billion (35 percent) gain to shareholders from retrenchment and return of resources to shareholders. Unocal paid out 52 percent of its equity by repurchasing stock with a $4.2 billion debt issue and reduced costs and capital expenditures.

CHAPTER 8   Taxes and Firm Value

1. See Roger J. Grabowski, "S Corporation Valuations in the Post-Gross World," *Business Valuation Review,* September 2002, pp. 128–141.

2. See *Gross v. Commissioner.*

3. The after-tax cost of capital is equal to the before-tax cost of capital multiplied by 1 minus the tax rate. Thus a 20 percent after-tax cost of capital is equivalent to a before-tax cost of capital of approximately 33 percent if the tax rate is 40 percent [20% ÷ (1 − 0.4) = 33.33%].

4. The analysis presented in this section is based on Scholes, Wolfson, Erickson Maydew, and Shevlin's book, *Taxes and Business Strategy: A Planning Approach*, 2nd ed., Prentice Hall.

5. The example used in the text is taken from Scholes et al., *Taxes and Business Strategy*, 2nd ed., p. 378.

6. See Appendix 8A for the formulas used to calculate the acquirer's indifference price shown in Table 8.4.

7. Merle Erickson and Shiing-wu Wang, "The Effect of Organizational Form on Acquisition Price," University of Chicago working paper, May 2, 2002.

CHAPTER 9 Valuation and Financial Reports: The Case of Measuring Goodwill Impairment

1. FAS 142 uses the term *fair value* and defines it as the amount at which an asset (or liability) could be bought (or incurred) or sold (or settled) in a current transaction between willing parties, other than in a forced or liquidation sale. This value standard is equivalent to the fair market value standard, which states that *fair market value* is the price a willing buyer will pay a willing seller when each is fully informed of the relevant facts and each is under no compulsion to transact.

2. Refer to FAS 142, paragraph 28.

3. By definition, the fair market value of a reporting unit equals the fair market value of net assets (fair market value of assets minus fair market value of liabilities) plus fair market value of implied goodwill plus the fair market value of liabilities. Thus, the implied fair market value of goodwill can also be calculated as the difference between the fair market value of the reporting unit and the aggregated fair market value of its assets. The FASB routinely describes the cost of acquiring in net terms—that is, transaction price less liabilities assumed. This is confusing from a valuation perspective since the cost of an acquisition reflects the value of assets purchased. How the acquisition was financed, on the other hand, is an important but separate matter.

4. For purposes of defining reporting units, an *operating segment* is defined in paragraph 10 of FAS 131, *Disclosures about Segments of an Enterprise and Related Information*.

5. Refer to FAS 142, paragraph 19.

6. In FAS 142, the term *value of operating unit* means value of the operating unit's equity and not the unit's total market value.

7. Refer to FAS 142, paragraph 23, footnote 16, p. 9.

8. FAS 142, B 155, p. 73.

9. U-Bid and eBay are examples of Internet sites that offer transaction information for many types of generic business equipment. However, for more specialized equipment, a secondhand market will generally not be available.

10. FAS 141, paragraph A14, p. 27, states that "assets designated by the symbol (₣) are those that would be recognized apart from goodwill because they meet the contractual legal criterion even if they do not meet the separability criterion. Assets designated by the symbol (▲) do not arise from contractual or other legal rights, but shall nonetheless be recognized apart from goodwill because they meet the separability criterion. The determination of whether a specific intangible asset meets the criteria in this Statement for recognition apart from goodwill shall be based on the facts and circumstances of each individual business combination."

Index